Mastering Your Data

Master Data Management

By Andy Graham

Published by Koios Associates Ltd

Copyright © 2015 by Koios Associates Ltd

Table of Contents

Contents

vi

Table of Figures

Table of Figures

Preface

Master data management has become a whole industry within an industry. There are many companies now claiming to be MDM software (or services) providers. Everyone wants a master data project on their CV and in general it has become hip and trendy (as trendy as enterprise IT ever gets). The problem is that, as with most IT band wagons, the truth of what is actually behind the terminology gets lost. I have looked at the current set of literature on the market and felt there was space for me to put my two pennies worth in. This book contributes to the MDM industry by providing my own views and experience in this space, and hopefully provides a little clarity.

This book is an attempt to capture this knowledge so that a wider audience can take advantage of it. I have described the salient points and provided a generic framework which can be tailored to fit the readers own organisation.

This book has been a bit of a voyage of exploration. It's taken far longer than I ever expected to write. This is partly due to the hectic nature of life both personal and work, and also because it's forced a certain level of learning in myself around this subject; as I realise there where bits I clearly didn't know enough about.

For those of you wondering about the picture on the front cover it is of the PETRONAS Twin Towers in Kuala Lumpur. Soaring 451.9 metres into the sky, this 88-storey twin structure is the crown jewel of Kuala Lumpur. It was taken whilst on holiday in Malaysia during 2013, and has been chosen as it represents an architectural wonder. The PETRONAS Towers demonstrate a mastery of the environment and I felt this to be fitting as I am writing about another type of architectural mastery; in this case data.

The intended audience of this text include data professionals, managers of data professionals, project/program managers, IT architects of all kinds and business analysts. There are also a number of chapters, specifically chapters 1, 3, 5 and 13, which will be of interest to the executive levels within an organisation.

This book covers a range of subjects within the master data management world. There are 13 chapters and 4 appendices:

- **Chapter 1 – Here be Monsters**: The book starts with a general overview of the reason why master data management is important and the history of where it has come from.
- **Chapter 2 – What is Master Data**: We next look at what is master data and how to spot it within your organisation.
- **Chapter 3 – The Business Case for MDM**: This chapter looks at the business drivers and some of the fundamentals that comprise the MDM business case. In effect this is the show me the money chapter.
- **Chapter 4 – Architecture, Principles and Concepts**: This chapter is an architectural breakdown of what constitutes an MDM system. It provides us with a basic reference architecture with which to explore the MDM world.

- **Chapter 5 – Master Data is Risky:** master data has inherent risks associated with it. This chapter looks at what those are and some of the approaches to mitigation.
- **Chapter 6 – Magnum Opus:** One of the key achievements for the MDM architect is the creation of the gold record. Behind this concept is the identification of the data sources that make it up. This chapter gives us a good grounding in the concept.
- **Chapter 7 – It's a Huge Job:** This chapter looks at how we find all the master data and keep this information up to date, without having to employ the world.
- **Chapter 8 – The Hub:** The master data hub is an important concept to understand and is in fact central to most MDM technologies. This chapter takes a look at this idea.
- **Chapter 9 – The Cross Walk:** This chapter looks at the challenges faced when using different reference systems and how to address them.
- **Chapter 10 – Identity Management:** With this chapter we examine some of the practicalities of identifies and how to manage them.
- **Chapter 11 – Record Linkage:** How do we bring data together from different systems and create a single harmonised record. This chapter addresses this difficult problem by looking at the techniques and processes involved.
- **Chapter 12 – The Challenges of Global MDM:** We live in a global world and therefore our approach to MDM needs to be mindful of this and handle the nuances of different parts of the globe.

- **Chapter 13 – Project Challenges:** The final chapter looks at the challenges associated with successfully instigating a MDM initiative.
- **Appendix 1 – References:** Throughout the book there our references indicated that are explained within this appendix. They can be spotted by the number within square brackets next to the associated text.
- **Appendix 2 – Fuzzy Matching Algorithms:** A series of short explanation of different fuzzy matching algorithms.
- **Appendix 3 – The Silk Road Story:** A story that puts a non-technical explanation to MDM.

I have used the word 'system' a few times within this book and a short explanation of what I mean by it is probably in order. A 'system' doesn't have to be technology based. When we think of systems, it is fair to say, we typically will be referring to a technology based process but they can also represent a human based process or system. When I refer to a system, I am referring to either and both together.

As I explained in my first book on the enterprise data model I am British and therefore the non-British readers will notice a few differences in spelling. Examples of this include 'organisation' (not organization) and 'modelling' (not modeling).

I hope this text provides value to the reader and I would welcome any feedback.

Andy Graham

www.koios-associates.com

About the author

Andy Graham is an experienced thought leader in the field of data and information architecture. Andy is Head of Data Architecture for HSBC's commercial banking arm. In his spare time he writes, publishes and does a little bit of training through his own company Koios Associates.

Formerly, Andy was Head of Enterprise Data Architecture at IMS Health where he provided leadership in the area of data architecture. Prior to this Andy worked as the Regional Manager of Sybase's Northern European Business Intelligence organisation. While at Sybase, he played a key role in building the BI organisation across EMEA and was instrumental in the delivery of many successful enterprise information solutions.

Andy has also worked for Hummingbird (formally Andyne) as the UK Consultancy Manager, where he was responsible for the development of a full spectrum of professional services to complement the companies' software offerings.

Andy started his data management career at Business Objects, where he was one of the founding members of the UK organisation and as such was responsible for the success of many customer implementations and information strategies.

Acknowledgements

As always with writing books it doesn't happen in a vacuum and there are many people that have contributed knowingly and unknowingly. First of all I would like to thank my partner Angela: she is, as always, an amazing support as I work through developing this text. Her assistance from an editorial support perspective (with her new found skills in this area) have also been priceless.

Next we have the many companies I have worked with over the years, including HSBC, IMS Health, BG Group, BAT, AXA, The Pension Regulator, Sybase, Hummingbird and Business Objects. There are also the many attendees on my data architecture course. These poor souls will have heard me banging on about the value of data architecture and MDM

1. Here be Monsters

Since the dawn of time, mankind has had a superstitious fear of the oceans. The sea could smash to pieces any ship that dared to sail on it, never to be heard of again. The oceans were an unknown, (still are to a degree) and what lived in them was also a terrifying mystery.

Figure 1 - Old Map with Sea Monsters

Many old maps contained sea monsters in the unexplored regions of the sea. As recently as the mid 1800's sea charts were still being illustrated with mythical and fearsome sea-creatures. They served to deter and obscure as well as fill in empty space on the maps [1].

This fear was very real, for example when Columbus was recruiting for his voyage of discovery to the America's he had difficulties in getting sailors to sign up due to the stories told by other seamen. He had to resort to using widely exaggerated promises of wealth to get the crew he needed for the trip.

Even in today's high tech world, where we are exploring space and the sub-atomic worlds, the oceans still holds dangers and secrets. Some of the weirdest creatures and natural formations on our planet can be found beneath the waves, and we're still finding more.

The reason for starting this book with a history lesson is that data is like an ocean, organisations have vast amounts of it just as our planet has oceans full of water. This sense of vastness and unknown horror is quite a good analogy to the typical organisational data landscape.

In a previous book I used quotes from both the poem 'Rime of the Ancient Mariner' by the English poet Samuel Taylor Coleridge and the 2008 UN Secretary General, Ban Ki Moon about water availability to relate data and water. In essence Ban Ki Moon remarked that water scarcity has the potential to fuel wars and conflict. This was based on some scary facts about water availability and consumption. Water constitutes about three quarters of the earth's surface, but only less than one percent of it can be used by its inhabitants; 97% is salt water and a further 2% is contained in glaciers. This is not unlike the situation we find in today's data rich but information poor organisations. We have vast amounts of data but only a small percentage of it is usable.

Data has become the life blood of business success and competitive advantage. Organisations varying from large multi nationals to local government departments or agencies use data to understand their business, marketplace and customers, so as to gain valuable business insight. Like the oceans the data landscape is vast and largely unknown by the companies that harbour it; in fact most organisations don't realise the real state of play of their data.

For all the highly skilled technologists that work at these companies, there are still challenges that make this an incredibly difficult mountain to climb. Underpinning all the data is fantastical technology that allows access to the data, or wizzies it around the global at tremendous speeds. Regardless of the amazing technology advancements that have been made, we are still faced with the challenge of making sure the data we are using is correct and means what we think it means.

Data Disconnect

So why do we have such a disconnected data world? There are a number of reasons for this so let's take a look at each of the key causes.

Shadow IT Organisations

The first one to mention is the shadow IT organisation. Central IT functions can often work at glacial speeds (costs can also be higher) and the business side of organisations typically struggle to understand or appreciate the lack of responsiveness. This means that it's all too common to find small IT teams springing up in the individual business units. This is done for a number of reasons; in an effort to speed up development, to try and reduce the costs or possibly to provide a degree of control over the departments own destiny. However, whatever the reason, trying to maintain consistency in the way data is handled across departments is normally compromised.

Mergers and Acquisitions

Mergers and acquisitions are part of corporate life. In fact they also occur in government and the 'not for profit world': sometimes government departments merge and it's also common for their responsibilities to get re-allocated.

Mergers and acquisitions are a massive undertaking when it comes to IT, but they are nearly always not completely finished. It is typical to find that a company which has gone through a number of mergers and acquisitions will have duplicate systems and or processes. This means, for example, you could find that a highly acquisitional company creates customer records in more than one place, as it has never integrated all the customer management systems. You would expect that the two (or more) systems are not checking to see if they have duplication of details. Just think of the potential for your customer addresses to be unsynchronised.

In reality companies normally end up with a mixture of integrated systems, part integrated and some with no integration at all.

COTS Products

Thirdly we have vendor software packages. It is common place for organisations to purchase COTS (Commercial Off The Shelf) software products. This means that rather than design and build a new customer service application or an accountancy system themselves a company will often purchase the complete package from a software vendor. This makes ample sense from a risk mitigation, timeline and cost perspective. Packages are generally cheaper to implement and have less risk associated with their development. This is because they already exist and are just being customised/tailored. This also makes them generally quicker to implement.

The problem here though is that each of these systems is likely to contain a degree of overlapping data. Let's take for example a customer services system, a sales management system and an accounts system. In each case we are likely to have data about customers, sales and products ordered. They may not be defined in exactly the same way or used in the same way or hold exactly the same data but in essence the same data is being used in multiple places.

- The sales management system will have details of contacts, their importance in signing off or agreeing to the proposed deal, forecast details, product, discounts and revenue amounts.
- The accounts system will have details of the customer's contacts from a payment perspective, actual financial transaction amounts and dates and product.
- The customer service system will have details about the customer contacts as regards service level agreements and support calls, product bugs and defect details and work-a-rounds.

Often there is a problem where the data overlaps. This is because unless these systems have significant integration, we are likely to have different versions of the same data.

Differences in Experience and Expectations

The individuals that work in organisations have varied backgrounds, be they cultural, educational or technological. One person may be used to using a large CRM system for managing customer data whilst a second may be used to using a localised PC database (like Microsoft Access) and/or spreadsheets software (like Microsoft Excel). This second group of users generally create complex processes to handle the various challenges associated with customer data. Across organisations that work in this way, it becomes hard to find uniformity in the way that data problems and complexity are handled. This leads then to data fragmentation and dispersal.

Lack of Glamour

Let's be honest, data is seen as unglamorous and 'in the weeds'. The typical stereotype of a data professional is not that flattering! This lack of glamour means that data often doesn't get the attention it deserves. It can suffer from a lack of attention from the 'C' level within the organisation which in turn can lead to a lack of investment. Data is not too dissimilar to the foundations of a house; no one sees it until something goes wrong!

Difficulties in Actually doing the Work

Data is complex stuff and the people who specialise in this area are often quite detailed in nature. They can therefore be lacking in the more architectural skill set, as often they have come from a heavily development or DBA focused role. Most data professionals look at the detail and fail to step back and understand the wider context that the data exists within. This stuff is complex to get your head around.

The Challenges of Data Fragmentation

We have so far looked at how data can be fragmented across the enterprise, but what impact does this actually have?

Increased Costs

Data fragmentation can increase the organisations cost base for a number of reasons such as:

- The extra process required to handle the fragmentation needs a greater IT footprint which in turn requires resource to manage.
- Fragmented data introduces data quality problems which need to be rectified or worked around, and this all means extra effort and processing.
- The use of Data Warehousing solutions to address the problem. These projects are large, complex (because of this fragmentation) and therefore costly and ultimately only mask the problem as it is still there in the operational systems.

Reduced Business Agility

It is important for businesses to be agile so that they can react to customer or market place pressures. Data Fragmentation causes extra processing, projects and technology which in turn reduces the companies' agility and therefore hurts the business. This is because every project requires many of the same data quality and integration challenges to be overcome, this adds time and cost to any initiative as we solve the same problems again and again.

Fragmented data introduces data quality problems … and this all means extra effort and processing.

Bad Decision Making

Bad or inconsistent data results in bad or inconsistent decision making. It should be obvious to the reader that having correct data underpinning business decisions, gives you a greater chance of success. Imagine launching an initiative to focus sales effort in France, because market trending data shows this is a major growth area, only to find out a year later (after a huge investment of money) that this data was incorrect. This is not only a massive waste of money but also a lost opportunity to use it on other initiatives. Having correct data allows the management team to make decisions based on facts. This then reduces risk, as decisions are based on a firm foundation.

What is MDM

It is now probably time to introduce the concept of MDM, as this is the subject that this book is all about. Master Data is a term used to describe an organisations core business data. Data such as customer records, product details, employee, supplier and location would typically represent master data. This data is considered critical to the successful running of the organisation.

Master Data Management, or MDM for short, is both a strategic and, I would argue, a practical approach that allows organisations to develop and maintain a consistent view of their master data. This may involve data that is scattered across a range of applications, although it is typically manufactured, or mastered in one place and distributed across the organisation.

It is, in reality, the reincarnation of the problem of how to manage the consistency and integrity of the myriads of data assets that exist across the enterprise. Systems such as ERP, SCM, CRM, BPM, ODS, data warehouses/marts, legacy applications, ECM (unstructured content like emails, documents, etc), portals and various home-grown applications. Each of these applications generates and works on a data set which partially or completely overlaps with the others. The same Customer, Product etc is often represented in two or more applications, sometimes differently. The objective of MDM can be therefore summarised as providing a consistent view of an organisations dispersed data and its associated definitions.

Master Data has Value

Master data is often one of the key assets of a business. It is not unusual for a company to be acquired primarily for access to its customer master data. There are also a number of companies that have created highly lucrative business models based on selling data about specific marketplaces (examples include: Reuters, Bloomberg, IMS Health, Aimia, and Dun & Bradstreet).

Over the last few decades commerce has changed from being biased towards tangible assets (such as factories, stock, property and physical products) to more intangible assets (such as intellectual property, marketing brands, IT systems and the data that resides in them). In essence, intangible assets have supplanted tangible assets as the key value drivers in today's economy.

Master data is often one of the key assets of a company.

The classification of intangible assets is in its infancy. Based on the current research in this area four areas of intangible assets can be identified:

- Knowledge: intellectual property (patents, recipes, product research), industry experience and knowledge (such as manufacturing and operating guides and manuals), IT systems and the data that resides in them.
- Business Processes: innovative business models, manufacturing techniques and supply chain operations.
- Market Positioning: contracts, distribution rights, licences (eg third generation telecom licences), import quotas, government permits etc.
- Brand and Relationship: trade names, trademarks and trade symbols, domain names, design rights, trade dress, packaging, copyrights and the brand relationship with the consumer.

Some examples of real world companies that have business models based on (or heavily impacted by) intangible assets are:

- Google purchased Motorola Mobility Holdings for over $12 billion to forestall patent litigation and force settlements with Apple Inc. (AAPL) and Microsoft Corp. (MSFT) over smartphone technology.
- ARM Holdings, a circa $1 billion company, is the world's leading semiconductor intellectual property (IP) supplier.

- Dun & Bradstreet is the one of the world's leading source of business information and insight for credit risk management, sales & marketing, supply management and regulatory compliance decisions worldwide. They have a huge commercial database containing more than 202 million business records.
- IMS Health gathers and connect more than 10 petabytes of complex healthcare data on diseases, treatments, costs and outcomes. This data is sold to pharmaceutical and healthcare organisations as well as government agencies.

The purpose of valuing the organisation's enterprise data is not about getting the exact value (if this is at all measurable) but to give a sense of the importance of this type of data to the organisation. It is easier to manage and understand things that can be valued rather than nebulous data concepts.

History of MDM

MDM is not new; it has been evolving as a distinct technology since the Mid 90's. In fact its roots stem from two distinctly different but also highly similar problems that face organisations: product data management and customer data management. Product Information Management (PIM) systems look at bringing all the product data into a single view of product, whilst on the customer side there is technology such as Customer Data Integration (CDI) and Customer Relationship Management (CRM) that aims to bring all the customer data into a single view.

PIM

PIM technology manages the data required to manufacture, market and sell products. It focuses on a centrally managed single view of product that feeds multiple systems such as product catalogues (be they paper based, web based or others), ERP systems and third parties. The types of data managed by a PIM system could be product descriptions, pricing info (used in product catalogues) or possibly size and weight details. The data held in all these systems needs to be up-to-date, correct and consistent.

The need for these types of systems grew because product data was (and still is to some degree) typically scattered across different departments, geographies and systems. You will find product data in systems such as CRM, ERP data warehouses, accountancy systems and spreadsheets.

The concept of PIM only started to gain board market acceptance in the early 2000s. Typically they are used by medium to large scale companies with one or more of the following characteristics:

- A wide range of products or permutations of products.
- Frequently changing products.
- A fragmented IT landscape.
- A large online business presence.
- A varied and complex channel mix.

CDI and CRM

CDI is a fundamental element of CRM technology and came into mainstream use in the 1990's. In essence it is the process of managing customer data from across the organisations IT systems; including contact details, customer purchases etc. Successful CDI means that all parts of the organisation have access to the most up to date and consistent set of customer data, i.e. a single view of the customer is made available throughout the organisation.

A special nuance of CDI is the identification of customer records across different systems and the bringing together of that data. We will discuss this further in chapters 10 and 11 but in summary it is full of problems. Take for example the simple situation of my name and how it could be represented in a number of different systems across an organisation. The table below shows a few of the options:

Andy Graham	
A Graham	Very confusing because my son has the same first initial as me. In fact the 'A' could stand for Alex, Adam, Aran etc.
Andrew Graham	The computer would need a rule to know that Andy and Andrew are the same.

Figure 2 - Example of how a name can be represented differently

Hopefully the reader can see that by using these three very simple and common versions of my name, it can be challenging distinguishing between them. In fact just a person's name can be made up of quite a few pieces of data when you actually break it down; for example family name, given name, alias, nick name, professional titles etc.

In addition to the complexity of name, we have complexity with addresses and various other formal (and less formal) identifiers such as email, phone numbers, account numbers, passport numbers and social security numbers. As mentioned earlier the whole situation is very challenging.

The concept of CDI started to gain traction in the late 1990's and then got merged into the whole CRM band wagon started by Rogers and Peppers.

Single View

It is worth pointing out, to avoid confusion, that when we talk about single view this doesn't really mean that there is only one single view of customer or product data. It actually means a single source of data that users and systems can access with differing perspectives. Users only see data that is relevant to them whilst at all times there is consistency across the different views, or slices, of data. To complicate matters even further, the single source doesn't have to be a physical single source; it can be a logical concept whereas physically it could be federated across a number of servers. But it is easier and more generally understood to say just 'Single View'.

ERP

Enterprise resource planning systems (ERP) store and manage data from across the business; such as manufacturing, supply chain and sales data. The ERP system in-effect allows the integration and sharing of data across these multiple departments.

The term was first used in the early 1990s and comes from a primarily (although not exclusively) manufacturing background. Initially these systems where concerned with back office functions that did not directly affect customers. Later front office functions, such as CRM, SRM (supplier relationship management) became integrated.

Figure 3 - Timeline for MDM technology

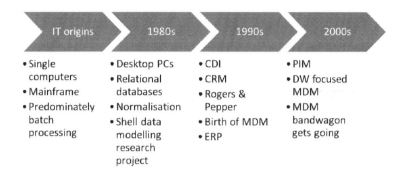

IT origins	1980s	1990s	2000s
• Single computers • Mainframe • Predominately batch processing	• Desktop PCs • Relational databases • Normalisation • Shell data modelling research project	• CDI • CRM • Rogers & Pepper • Birth of MDM • ERP	• PIM • DW focused MDM • MDM bandwagon gets going

ERP in my humble opinion is another attempt to address the MDM problem by making the whole world conform to one version of reality.

Data Warehouse focused MDM

Data Warehousing MDM is basically a MDM system that solves the ETL challenges that underpin data warehousing. Challenges such as data quality, data transformations and data record linkage. The main vendor in this space (at the time of writing) is probably Kalido which started life in 1985 as a research project within the Royal Dutch/Shell Group. Between 1997 and 2000, the software was developed and born. One of the capabilities Kalido has always claimed to have is the ability to act as a MDM hub primarily for use by data warehouse implementations. I am sure I'll get calls from various sales people telling me it does far, far more than that (and I am sure it does) but the point is that this is where its MDM origins started.

Summary

In this chapter we have introduced the concept of master data and MDM. We have explored the reasons why companies need MDM and the history behind the evolution of this approach.

So what really is master data and master data management. Master data can be considered to be the organisations core business data for example customer, product and supplier. Master data Management can be considered to be a disciple for the management of an organisations core (master) data. The objective of MDM is to provide, and maintain, a consistent view of an organisations core business data.

A few closing points on this chapter that are worth making:

- Like most organisational challenges in today's world, it involves the triad (people, process and technology). It is so important to recognise that MDM is more than just technology.
- It is in effect the reincarnation of an old problem.
- It's interesting to listen to the subtext when discussing MDM with software vendors. If you listen carefully you can understand where their particular technology started (PIM, CDI, DW, etc).

2. What is Master Data?

So what is master data? How can we spot it? What does it look like? There is a widely shared view that Master Data is just reference data. This is not nearly specific enough; it just condemns us to a generic approach to MDM. Within this chapter we will address the question of what master data is and how to identify it.

What is Data?

The place to start is by explaining what we mean by the term data. Data can best be described as individual facts that have a specific meaning for a given time period. It can be at the atomic level (for example 'date of birth') or derived (such as 'age'). Therefore, if we take a person called John Smith who is born on the 1st September 1999 we have three pieces of atomic data (first name, surname and date of birth) and two pieces of derived data (full name and age). The full name is a combination of the first and surname whilst the age is derived from the date of birth.

Data can be considered as the basic building blocks used to create information; as on its own it has no meaning. For data to become information, it must be interpreted and take on meaning. Information therefore can be defined as data that has been collected together to create some type of larger context than the individual pieces of data themselves.

How do we Identify Master Data?

The three high level distinguishing characteristics of master data that will help you identify it are that it:

1. Is not transactional, but it's used by and linked to transactions so as to provide context and meaning to them. A bunch of dates and numbers are meaningless without knowing which customer or product they are associated with.

2. Is of known provenance. It's of no value to the organisation if we don't know how reliable our master data is and where it comes from.

3. Has value and meaning independent of transactional data.

The Different Types of Master Data

Now that we have identified our master data, we need to drill a little further and understand the different types of master data we are dealing with; as this will affect both its behaviour and how we manage it.

Master data can be sub divided into four distinct classifications which are:

- Reference Data

- Transaction Structure Data

- Enterprise Structure Data

- Enterprise Metadata

Reference Data

Reference Data is any kind of data that is used to categorise other data found in a database. Alternatively it can be used to relate data in a database to information beyond the boundaries of the organisation. This type of data is also known as: Lookup Data, Domain Values or just Codes and Descriptions.

ISO 3166-1-alpha-2 code	Country name
AF	AFGHANISTAN
AX	ÅLAND ISLANDS
AL	ALBANIA
DZ	ALGERIA
AS	AMERICAN SAMOA
AD	ANDORRA
AO	ANGOLA

Figure 4 - ISO 316 country code and short name standards

A good example of reference data are country codes and names. Transaction records may be tagged with the country that they occurred within. The actual definition and values for a country are typically not defined by the organisation whose transactional data is being tagged, but instead is defined outside

19

by a governing body (in this case the ISO standards body). In figure 4 our example shows a sample of the ISO codes and names for countries. This list is sourced from the ISO standards body which in turn is sourced from the United Nations.

Reference data has the following characteristics:

- It only has a few rows and columns so it only need a small amount of storage.
- It is not normally covered by data privacy legislation or commercial sensitivity.
- In some cases it can be re-created quite easily. An example would be the ISO country list which can be just reloaded from source.
- Sometimes the origins of this data can be external.
- It is simple in structure. A simple domain database structure may be enough to store all this type of data.
- It can be challenging to link across different reference systems for the same thing.
- It is very slowly changing. For example, a currency list or country list is likely to change very irregularly. To illustrate this, from 2000 to 2010 only the following new countries have been born:
    - May 20, 2002 - East Timor declares independence from Indonesia.
    - 2003 – The Union of Serbia and Montenegro was voted in by its parliament.
    - 2006 - Serbia and Montenegro split.
    - 2008 - Kosovo declared independence from Serbia.
    - 2011 - South Sudan gained independence after a referendum that followed on from a 2005 peace agreement.

Transaction Structure Data/Core Business Data

This is data that represents the direct participants in a transaction, and which must be present before a transaction can be fully understood e.g. Customer, Product and Supplier. This data is often considered as the businesses core data. Transactions typically need to be related to this type of data, so as to give the transaction some meaning and purpose.

Without transaction structure data, there would be severe consequences for the organisation in question. Imagine what would happen to a bank if it lost or had corrupted some (or all) of its customer data, or the consequences of not knowing which deposits related to which bank account.

Characteristics are:

- Data privacy or possible commercial sensitivity are important with some transaction structure data (customer details as an example).
- The data has huge impact on the business if lost or corrupted. This potentially can result in the business being unable to function.
- It has commercial value in its own right – i.e. customer contact details can have a financial value as they can be sold or are possibly the reason a company is purchased.
- Sometimes the origins of this data can be external, for example product data may be provided by the product manufacturer.

Enterprise Structure Data

Enterprise structure data is data that describes the important structures that exist within the organisation, more commonly referred to as 'hierarchies'. It permits business activity to be reported or analysed by business functions or by product grouping. Within our enterprise structure data we would expect to have enough data to be able to explain the hierarchy to any consuming system.

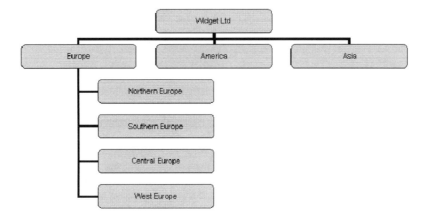

Figure 5 - Widget Ltd organisation structure

Characteristics are:

- This data affects how the organisation understands itself or the things it does (and sells). Without it the long-term viability of the business is questionable as dis-organisation will be rife.
- Parent child relationships inherent within any hierarchy allow us to navigate through the hierarchical tree structure.
- Multiple hierarchies can be a common occurrence.
- Each node in the hierarchy normally represents a piece of transaction structure data although it can also be

reference data in the case of a diagnosis classification system.

- Typically this type of master data is internally created.

Enterprise Metadata

Metadata is often referred to as data about data; this means it is data that describes other types of data such as the structure of a database. It is often found in a database's system catalogue and sometimes included in database table definitions. Metadata is not directly used to run or manage the enterprise. It is often used by IT staff to assist them in their work, or business users to help them use IT resources.

One often overlooked aspect of metadata is that it is not just "data about data". It can, for example, include descriptions of networks or may represent a set of business rules used by an application. An example of metadata would be the definition of a data element such as Product Reference Number or Customer Status.

In the context of master data we are referring to metadata that is used across multiple systems (rather than the metadata used to manage a single discrete system) or metadata that defines our master data.

Characteristics are that it:

- Enhances our understanding (such as a description) of one of the other master data types. By this I mean that it either defines structure, descriptions or rules about other data.
- Is is shared between applications. Some meta data is not shared and is internal to the system but we are not interested in this type of meta data. The shared version only is enterprise master data.

What Master Data is Not

This whole chapter has been about defining what master data is but it can sometimes be just as helpful to understand what it is not and why. There are three categories of data that are not master data: transaction activity data, transaction audit data and non enterprise wide metadata.

Transaction Activity Data

This is data that represents the operations (actual business transactions) that the company carries out; such as dates and amounts. Examples would be:

- Dates of invoices and the amounts for each line item
- Dates of customer meetings and events
- Dates that geological measurements are taken

Transaction Activity Data is not master data because it is by its very nature transactional.

Transaction Audit Data

This is data that tracks the life cycle of individual transactions such as audit trails and server logs. This is typically found within individual systems (for providing auditing on that system) and therefore is not master data.

Non Enterprise Metadata

The characteristics that define this type of metadata are:

- It is typically internal to a system and used to make that system function and therefore issues with this data will affect the usability of the system.

- It has no value outside the system, in the wider enterprise.

Summary

It is important to be able to understand the characteristics of different types of master data. This chapter looks at classifying master data so that we can be far more refined in our understanding and treatment of the differences of master data. For example, we have seen that transaction structure data is highly critical to an organisation and should have far greater levels of resources allocated to it compared to over types of master data. Lastly the chapter has provided us with the knowledge to spot master data; as we have defined its characteristics.

3. The Business Case for MDM

Before embarking on an MDM programme it is imperative that we can justify the investment required. The organisational investment phase (ie business case) is a critical stage in securing executive management commitment and organisational buy-in and therefore warrants a whole chapter to its self.

Over the years I have encountered numerous companies that have looked at instigating an MDM initiative. This has often gone on for many years, but never got off the ground due to an inability to build a justifiable business case or develop a common vision across the organisation to justify the investment. This failure to progress has consequences including the cost of time spent chasing a non-existent dream and the advantages enjoyed by competitors who are able to make use of such technology to achieve competitive advantages. It can also have reputation consequences for those involved, as they will be tarred with this failure.

In this chapter we will address questions such as:

- Why should your organisation be investing in MDM?

- What is the business driver behind this type of investment?
- How do I express the business value?

Business Drivers

MDM is not a term that many business executives will be familiar with or understand, and why should they. Often an MDM initiative will be run under another name such as 'Single View of Customer', 'Single View of Product' or 'Patient Electronic Records System'. Executives may (or may not) realise this is MDM under the guise of another name. The reality of the situation is that I don't think it is important; what matters are results. I've worked with one client who, for years, developed and rolled out a MDM hub but referred to it as a reference repository due to organisational political pressure. Over the years, with various rounds of managerial changes, the name gradually changed and now this solution is referred to as a MDM hub openly. This process took three years and three directors!

Probably the first question faced will be the 'do we really have a problem at all' question. Most mature companies will have spent years building IT systems to support the business and on the surface all seems to work. The problem is that as IT professionals we have become experts in hiding the complexity and limitations of what we develop by cheap and nasty work-a-rounds. We have become so good at this that often the business has little idea of how bad the situation really is, as it all seems to work as far as they can see. Why should they therefore be interested in investing millions of dollars on a non-problem?

An organisations IT infrastructure is a bit like the infrastructure of a house; it evolves over time. When a house is built you get wonderful architecture plans that show you every nook and cranny. After a few years when you've had a new boiler put in or maybe a new bathroom, alarm system or turned one of the bedrooms into an en-suite the architecture drawings only show half the truth. Obviously some of the original architecture drawings will still be valid but lots of things will have changed and the original drawings are never updated and often the new changes are never written down anywhere. This is fine whilst you still live in the house as we have a memory, but bare a thought for the poor souls who buy the house from you 10 years later, and have no idea about these changes, let alone anything written down to tell them.

The problem is that as IT professionals we have become experts in hiding the complexity and limitations of what we develop by cheap and nasty work-a-rounds.

To make this problem real I will use an example from my own personal experience. In most residential properties in the UK there is a tap called a stop cock, which is used for turning off the water to a house. This tap is often inside the house - typically within the kitchen. It would be used in the case of a leak or if there was some plumbing work to do. My house on the other hand has no visible stop cock. This has resulted in a few interesting occurrences over the years. In the case of an emergency you have to leave the house and go out into the street and turn it off from the water mains. In fact there is a stop cock, but due to extensions to the property by previous owners, it has been built into a wall somewhere and I have no idea where! Extrapolate this problem out to the many infrastructure items within the typical organisation, then add in the level of complexity and you should start to get a sense of the problems faced by IT organisations.

Typically MDM initiative is driven (at least initially) from IT. This is probably because, as has been mentioned earlier, IT have hidden the problems from the business but are painfully aware themselves. This obviously has the challenge of the business not seeing the value. Therefore a project can look, if we are not careful, like a massive white elephant infrastructure project with no real identifiable business value and therefore it becomes doomed.

IT led engagements can't work, right? Well this doesn't need to be the case. IT often has a better broader grasp of the challenges facing the business as they need to work across departments and functions. Regardless of IT or business leadership we need to build the business case. So to develop our business case we need to understand the business drivers. These broadly fit into three camps; drivers that reduce costs, drivers that grow revenue, and intangible drivers that cannot be easily measured. To add to this, these drivers will vary depending on industry. Now let's look at some areas where MDM adds value to a business.

Company Mergers

We have already mentioned company mergers and acquisitions when we looked at the reasons for the data discount in the first chapter. One of the typical elements behind a M&A business case is cost synergies (or savings in plain speak).

IT integration is a critical part of any company merger or acquisition, because without it you have no opportunities for cross integration of the business or organisational controls. It therefore follows that an integration roadmap should be part of the plan when buying another company, as it informs to the cost of integration and reaching the projected cost savings. Get this wrong and the rational for the merger may not stack up. MDM should play a significant part in the M&A process, because the ability to hook up to a MDM hub as a way of integrating master data is a massive enabler to the cost saving agenda.

The other aspect to consider is that the operational efficiencies typically identified will be based on numbers provided from the systems being used in the company being acquired (and the acquiring company). If we have issues with the validity of these numbers then our cost savings are questionable. If you don't have the full picture how do you expect to fully understand the cost synergies associated with the merger or acquisition? It stands to reason that good master data results in improved realisation of M&A benefits.

The Customer

The traditional business goals of improving both customer service and customer experience have helped to drive the MDM market. The reason is that having complete and correct data about all of a customer's interactions with the business allow the company to gain valuable insight into the customer, their goals and the business opportunities that may exist for supporting those customer needs. Better knowledge of the customer equals:

- Better targeted products and offerings, which in turn means a higher success rate.
- Tailored services and improved customer experience. An improved understanding of the customers drivers and needs means we can offer more refined and generally improved customer service; resulting in increased recurring revenue.
- The ability to identify good and bad customers and therefore take appropriate action.
- Improved customer service levels. By having complete, consistent and correct master data, customer service personnel will not waste time looking for customer detail and customer history information. This in turn improves the throughput of customers that can be handled and also the quality of the customer interaction as the customer doesn't experience long delays.

MDM is fundamental to successful CRM, which has as its agenda the intent to get a complete 'Single View' of the customer. This is sometimes referred to as a '360 Degree View'. MDM is doing the same thing but with master data.

Figure 6 – 360° degree view

Business Intelligence and Data Warehousing

I've spent many years working in the business intelligence marketplace; first at BusinessObjects and then for a number of other vendors. The reliance of companies on information derived from this type of technology is massive, but all falls apart if the data underpinning it is not accurate or complete.

Typically we talk of slicing and dicing our measures by the dimensions in our data warehouse or cube. The underlying premise to this, which is often never spoken about, is that we have assumed the data in our dimension is correct and represents the full picture. Let's just imagine for a moment a few silly but still realistic scenarios, and consider the degradation in the value of the reports, analysis etc and the decisions that are made from them.

To put some of this into a more understandable form I have a few scenarios that should help:

- Scenario 1: The miss-spelling of data such as regions, countries and customer names would result in us having extra records in our dimensions. This in turn would result in reports looking odd, as records don't get grouped (or aggregated) correctly. It therefore becomes harder to fully understand the data. This can be got around by messing about with the data to fix it which clearly is a drain on resources. There is an important assumption behind this fix- that we realise the data is wrong in the first place.
- Scenario 2: Missing customer records means missed opportunities, as you can't sell to someone you know nothing about or cannot find. Also how do you allocate revenue or costs to customers that don't exist? A whole accounting reconciliation activity is likely to ensue.

- Scenario 3: What about if there was incorrect data about a customer. You believe that they are a highly successful and wealthy individual, or company, when in fact they are struggling to make ends meet or don't even fit your target market. This would result in you wasting valuable resources targeting them for something they don't need or cannot afford to buy!

Another consideration is that the challenges being resolving with MDM are common problems for data warehousing and the BI world. For example, typically the warehouse would manufacture various derived business values and would have responsibility for linking different data sets together into a single harmonised data set. You would generally expect that the largest proportion of the cost of your data warehouse is due to MDM style problems.

Data Integration

A typical organisation will have a spaghetti of integrated systems where the integration is typically point to point. Although hidden to the business (because it all works), there are hidden costs such as support, license fees, hardware and data quality issues caused by the different approaches to integration. A text book MDM implementation would be based on a hub architecture where the MDM hub would act as a central point for all integration to occur. Therefore the spaghetti would be removed.

Data Quality

I know we have already mentioned data quality under the umbrella of business intelligence and data warehousing but there is another side to it. The problem with data is that it degenerates over time. I've heard statistics such as 2% of customer records are obsolete during a month because of divorce, death, marriage or people moving house. Add to this internal issues, such as data entry errors and problems caused by systems migrations for examples, and you can end up with a large numbers of bad records.

Let's look at a simplistic direct marketing example to illustrate the point. The marketing department has a customer database of 100,000 customers, and 2% of the addresses have a problem (due to the data degradation just mentioned). There is a new product which the marketing department want to mail shot to this customer base. If we then assume a typical response ratio of something like 2%, and a cost per mail shot piece of £1, we get a breakdown as follows.

(A) Cost of each mail shot piece	£1
(B) The number of pieces mailed per marketing campaign.	100,000
(C) The cost of each marketing campaign. This is calculated as (A * B)	£100,000
(D) Typical conversion rate	2%
(E) Customers with incorrect addresses	2% = 2,000

Figure 7 - Table of campaign number break down

Based on these numbers and a product that retails at £150 we get a comparison that shows a difference per marketing campaign of £6,000.

The breakdown is shown in the table on the following page.

	With incorrect addresses	With addresses fixed
(F) Number of customers that are actually contacted (B – E)	98,000	100,000
(G) Number of customers that purchased the new product (F * D)	1,960	2,000
(H) Revenue from campaign (G * 150)	£294,000	£300,000
(I) Profit per campaign (H – C)	£194,000	£200,000

Figure 8 - Table showing business case

£6,000 is not a world shattering amount but if we then multiple this over a number of campaigns, and into the other areas of the organisation that use addresses, we can start to get a sensible figure for the impact of incorrect addresses. Combine this with the other data quality issues that probably exist in the data, such as duplicate customers and incorrect customer profiles, and we can get some sizable numbers.

Risk, Privacy, Compliance and Control

There has been lots of talk within organisations and the media of late around risk, data privacy and compliance. Can MDM help in this area? The answer is certainly yes. Take credit risk as an example. We can be more confident that we understand the customers complete exposure if we have:

- a single view of customer data across the entire organisation's different systems, rather than individual data silo's
- data that can be relied upon to be correct

Accurate records about customers, assets and products leads to greater chance of adherence to corporate principles, policies and standards. This is because real deviations can be identified and remedial action can (if required) be taken. This also leads to greater ability to comply with legal and regulatory compliance requirements such as Basel/Sarbanes-Oxley. The failure to adhere to such regulations can be financially devastating and sometimes may involve prison; as governments become more robust in their punishments for such breaches.

Chapter 5 explores this subject in greater detail.

Operational Efficiency

Badly managed master data impacts on an organisation's operational efficiency. For example the administrative overhead associated with redundant data entry can become noticeable. If you add up the amount of time staff spend in the pointless activity of keying in the same data into different systems, you will understand my point.

How much administrative time is spend fixing issues with orders being rejected because of an invalid customer or product or some other detail that is not correct. Often this is caused by the lack of a coherent master data strategy, and therefore the system that registers the customer hasn't updated the order entry system. This leads to a rejected order, as the order entry system does not know about the new customer yet.

As a consequence, there are increased costs of account setup and customer acquisition due to administrative overheads and duplication of activities/effort. Also the duplication of data entry leads to increased data entry errors and exceptions.

Business Agility

I've called this section business agility, but it could just as easily be called IT agility as it relates to the increase time, costs and risks associated with the changes to the IT infrastructure needed to support new business initiatives. For example, the integration of two or more IT systems and the reduction in errors/testing associated with that integration. A centralised, consolidated, cleaned, de-duplicated store of master data that can be leveraged by every new application/project, will dramatically reduce implementation time which in turn reduces the time to market of the associated business initiative.

MDM Use Cases

Different types of master data have different patterns in the way they are created, maintained and used across an organisation and this needs to be factored into our thinking. How you implement MDM is dependent upon what you are using it for. There are three key use cases that are prevalent, these are: operational, analytical and insight.

Operational Use Case

In this context MDM is used as a central point of integration for master data. This means that master data needs to be accessed by applications and users across the organisation. These applications and users will need to be able to access, modify and potentially create master data whilst maintaining the consistency of master data across the users/applications concerned. We can also have the need to support a collaborative environment where applications and users participate in the same process but with different roles or at different points in the process.

An example of this would be the creation of a product record. It would not seem unreasonable to assume that contributions will be required from product experts, marketing and the local sales operations in each geography that you intend to sell the product. The level of involvement from each of these actors will change depending on the stage in the product life cycle.

Analytical Use Case

In this context MDM is used as an analytical ready source of master data for the organisations warehouse and analytical systems. This reduces the costs associated with building a data warehouse, as a large proportion of them stem from the ETL activities required to transform and clean source data to be usable within the warehouse.

This can be taken a stage further, by feeding back into the MDM hub insight gained within the data warehouse so that it can be used by the wiser business. An example of this type of actionable intelligence could be customer value. By analysing the customer interactions stored in the warehouse we can determine the net value (revenue – cost). This value can then become an attribute within our customer master data.

Insight Use Case

With this style of use case we are looking at actually discovering insight from analysis of the companies master data itself. The process of providing a single view of customer, product or supplier master data provides many interesting opportunities. For example we could ask:

- How many customers changed address in the last year?

- How many new customers did we gain last month?
- Who has a relationship with customer X and why?
- Why is the quality of our customer address data poor?

The Business Case

It's now time to look at the business case piece. At a simplistic level a business case explains to the board of directors, or senior managers, what the return will be for investing a certain amount of money on an initiative. They will use this to decide which of the initiatives, they have under consideration, to invest in. Organisational budgets are not endless, and decisions need to be made as to what to spend that budget on. IT budgets for example typically have a high proportion dedicated to maintaining the current technology infrastructure. Therefore investment of budget needs to be considered based upon the most bangs for the buck.

A compelling business case would look at both the tangible (quantifiable) and intangible (unquantifiable) aspects of the initiative. The form and style of a business case will be dependent upon the organisation's culture. It is not appropriate for this book to dwell too much on the general content, but we will spend some time exploring the financial aspects as that is where the most problems occur in expressing the business case for MDM.

Techniques

This is not a book on accountancy and business case development, but I felt it is useful to provide the reader with an introduction to a few business case techniques. Obviously the usefulness of each will depend on the organisation you're working in, and the situation you find yourself in.

When I started writing this section I ended up reaching for a book from my small library of text books at home. The one in question is 'The 10 day MBA' by Steven Silbiger [2] which I read in the mid 90's. So I included below three techniques for measuring the viability of a project and used a few MDM examples to show how these techniques can be applied to MDM initiatives.

- Return on Investment (ROI)
- Cash Flow Analysis
- Net Present Value (NPV)

Return on Investment

ROI, or Return on Investment to give it its full name, is a simplistic way of representing the value an investment of money represents. The calculation is the benefit (or return) divided by the cost of the investment. To represent this as a calculation we get the following:

$ROI = (V - C)/C$

The value, or gain, (V) created by the investment minus the cost of the investment (C) and the divide this by the cost (C) of the investment to get a ratio.

To explain how this works let's take as an example two investment projects:

Investment Project A

This is an initiative to improve the quality of data. This programme has been estimated to save the company £2,000,000 of costs over the next 5 years. The price to implement this programme is estimated at £500,000. We therefore get the following:

ROI = (2,000,000 – 500,000)/500,000 = 3

Investment Project B

We also have a second project which is going to look at upgrading one of our data centres. The cost savings for this are projected to be £1,500,000 and the cost to rollout is £428,000. This gives us the following:

ROI = (1,500,000 – 428,000)/428,000 = 2.5

The ROI calculation shows, in a very simplistic way, that from a purely financial perspective project A is a more efficient use of the companies' funds. In general ROI is quite popular as a metric as it is simple and flexible and can be modified to suit your particular circumstances.

Cash Flow Analysis

This analysis looks at the cost of the investment and how much cash it will generate each year. This is important as cash can be used to pay off debt, fund other projects or purchase new assets. So using our data quality example with £2,000,000 of savings over the next 5 years, we would get the results shown in figure 9. I've assumed as part of this example that the cost savings actually occur in year 2 (1,000,000 cost saving), 3 and 4 (both with 500,000 cost savings).

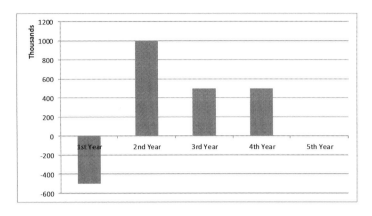

Figure 9 – Cash Flow for Project A

We can then compare this against our other project (see below) and find that the actual cash created is significantly lower and therefore has less 'financial value'.

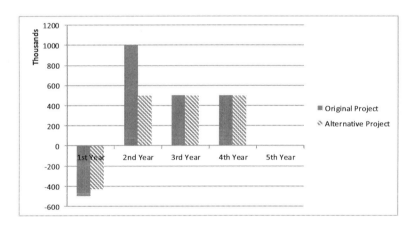

Figure 10 – Cash Flow Comparison of Project A + B

We can easily see that our original project A is far more financially beneficial to the company. With this type of analysis, you sometimes need to look at the cash flow accumulated value as well as some more sophisticated calculations for understanding cash flow.

Net Present Value (NPV)

NPV is used by accountants in capital budgeting analysis so that they can see, for any given project, how profitable it is likely to be. It compares the value of money today against the value of that money at some point in the future, by taking on board the effects of inflation and predicted income. If the NPV of a project is negative it means that the cash flow is likely to be negative as well and therefore you should probably reject the project. On the other hand, a positive NPV means the project should be accepted. It works by factoring the future savings by a discount value that represents inflation. The discount factors could be as follows:

		Discount Factor
Year 1 (start year)	£1	£1
Year 2	£1	£0.9
Year 3	£1	£0.8
Year 4	£1	£0.7
Year 5	£1	£0.6

Figure 11 – Discount Factor

Using our examples we get the following:

Year	Discount Factor	Project A		Project B	
		Cash	Cash in current terms	Cash	Cash in current terms
Year 1	1	(£500,000)	(£500,000)	(£428,000)	(£428,000)
Year 2	£0.9	£1,000,000	£900,000	£500,000	£450,000
Year 3	£0.8	£500,000	£400,000	£500,000	£400,000
Year 4	£0.7	£500,000	£350,000	£500,000	£350,000
Total			1,150,000		772,000

Figure 12 - Discount Factored applied to examples

So project A gives us £1.15 million whilst project B only gives us £0.772 million. It can quickly be seen that project A will provide a far greater level of profitability.

Metrics

A few quick words about metrics before we move onto the next chapter. It's important to be able to measure the successes of any MDM initiative, and to this end metrics should be maintained showing what has been achieved. These metrics can be driven out of the original business case, for example cost savings.

Summary

It's important to be able to explain the business reasons behind any investment in MDM. In this chapter we have looked at the business drivers behind the topic. We have covered such diverse drives such as: data quality, mergers and acquisitions, integration, and risk analysis. In the second half of the chapter we explored NPV, cash flow and ROI techniques for assessing value. We should now be equipped with the tools to start expressing the reasons behind our MDM initiative.

4. Architecture, Principles and Concepts

The intention of this chapter is to take an architectural look at MDM and to break it down into its constituent components. The transition to managing your organisation's master data effectively doesn't happen overnight. So when you 'do' MDM what bits do you need? What services or software components are required to support our Master Data endeavors? The chapter starts with a look at a general set of principles that underpin our work in the master data field. Then we will look at identifying each of the parts (or components) required within our MDM system. Please do remember that when I use the term system it can mean business or operational processes as well as software. It is important not to fall into the trap that everything about MDM must be fulfilled by technology.

Architectural Principles

Before looking at the technical components that makeup a MDM architecture, we need to understand the principles that provide the drivers for these components. Principles provide us with guidance and direction to operate within when developing or modify a system.

We will express each principle using a TOGAF notation i.e. Name, Statement, Rationale and Implications. TOGAF is a fairly standard notation for this kind of thing; and anyway I only a few years ago attended a TOGAF course so it would be wrong of me to ignore what was taught.

S.A.F.E.

There are four key principles which capture the core drivers for MDM. These can be summarised by the following four words: Security, Authority, Flexibility and the Enterprise. Taking these words and the first letter of each gives us an acronym SAFE (**S**ecurity, **A**uthority, **F**lexibility and **E**nterprise). The word SAFE is used here because it serves two purposes. Not only does it provide an acronym, but it also reminds us that unless we adhere to the underlying principles of the MDM architecture, the MDM component will become unsafe and will have inherent issues. So let's have a look at each of these principles in a little detail.

Principle 1- Security

Statement

Data security and privacy must be managed so as to fulfil commercial, legal and ethical needs and responsibilities.

Rationale

When companies make valuable master data available from one place, it can cause greater security and privacy issues than the organisation has previously faced. Data security and data privacy have become major issues over the last decade; due in part to the rise of the internet and internet based companies capturing all sorts of valuable data about people. There is legislation in place within most jurisdictions that mean companies can face massive fines for breaches. This ignores, obviously, the commercial impact of losing (or misusing) master data.

Implication

- Users (and interacting systems) are only allowed to access data that they have authority to access in the mode they have authority to work in.

- Data privacy issues need to be identified and managed as companies have legal responsibilities in this area.

- 3rd party data must be used and managed in accordance with any contractual arrangements.

Principle 2 - Authority

Statement

For master data to be valuable to an organisation it needs to have authority.

Rationale

For our MDM solution to be valuable to the organisation and treated as the single source, or golden source of truth, it needs to have authority. If users don't trust the data any MDM initiative will fail.

Implication

- Not only should we handle the dissemination of master data across the organisation, but we should disseminate data that everyone believes/knows is correct and has known providence.
- The master data should also have identifiable business value. There is no point in building an MDM system as a pure IT initiative as the value of master data is in its business usage.
- All master data must have an identified business owner. Ownership of data needs to be clear and managed through the system.
- The meaning of each piece of master data needs to be clear and unambiguous. This also implies that we should not take onboard master data we do not understand.
- Creation and modification of master data must conform to business rules and policies for master data.
- The quality of the data must be measured and articulated to the data consumers.

Principle 3 - Flexibility

Statement

Change is one of the only constants and this needs to be catered for.

Rationale

Organisations are inherently unstable. By this I mean that organisational structures, business goals, business drivers and the market place that organisational exists in are all in a state of flux. To top it all the technology that these organisations rely upon is constantly changing:

- Price/performance of all electronic devices doubles every 18-24 months

- Over a six year period from 1977 to 1982, Atari's home game business grew from $50 million to $1.6 billion in revenue

- Cisco and Bay Networks have appeared out of nowhere to become billion-dollar companies

- Hewlett-Packard's PC printer business, a $10 billion enterprise in 1994 shipped its first product only 10 years earlier

- Microsoft in less than 15 years grew from a boutique language software company to one of the richest and most powerful companies in the world.

It is reasonable then to expect any MDM architecture to have the flexibility to handle change.

Implications

Areas to consider are:

- The solution design should be able to handle change to master data, master data definitions, business needs and legal changes.

- It should make use of industry standards to ensure that the use of multiple technology (and changes in technology) can be accommodated. This will also ensure that the rollout is easier; as less pain will be felt integrating with the variety of vendor software packages that can typically be found across most organisations. Standards don't need to be technology based, they may also represent coding and interfaces.

- It should also be based on the concept of re-use. This means that sub components should be designed to be re-useable and also existing systems should be re-used within the MDM architecture if sensible.

- It should be possible to incrementally develop the MDM solution rather than have to embark on a big bang approach. This allows business value to be realised quickly whilst building towards the final end state.

- It should be decoupled. Master data is used throughout an organisation therefore it becomes important to create an architecture that can handle the variety of technologies and changes of technology both within the MDM environment and within the wider enterprise. Using a decoupled approach components (or services) can be integrated with each other and invoked by different applications for different uses, by different technology.

Principle 4 - Enterprise

Statement

A MDM component need to be designed with consideration for the whole of the enterprise.

51

Rationale

There is no point implementing a MDM architecture within part of an organisation (such as the marketing function) otherwise the whole business proposition starts to fall apart.

Implications

To this end there are a couple of points to consider:

- Only a single version of any master data must be made available. There is no point in having multiple customer masters as I'm not going to know which is correct or which to use? Master data is captured/created once and used multiple times.
- There should be consistency in the architecture. By this I mean that the architecture which is put in place will evolve, but that evolution should be in keeping with the long term vision rather than departmental initiatives with no overarching coordination.
- Master data needs to be governed as you would any other critical asset in the enterprise. The alternative would be information chaos and anarchy. Seriously, why would we bring together master data from all over the enterprise and not govern the decision-making process and results, it would be a value destruction exercise worthy of the Guinness Book of World Records.
- Master data is also enterprise data. Only data that has value across the organisation should be managed via the MDM system.

MDM Reference Architecture

Let's take a look at the architecture that underpins a typical MDM system. To do this we will make use of a reference architecture. A reference architecture provides a way of understanding the different capabilities we need, whilst at the same time it provides a common vocabulary with which to discuss implementations.

The diagram on the next page shows the key sub-components of our MDM reference architecture. The details behind each may vary, and the technology* will in all likelihood be different, however the core capabilities of each sub component are essential for a successful MDM system.

Our reference architecture is broken down into 5 distinct layers:

- Integration
- Data Management
- Data Quality
- Data Storage
- System Administration

* *The components in this architecture don't have to be implemented via technology; they can instead be implemented via business process (more about this later).*

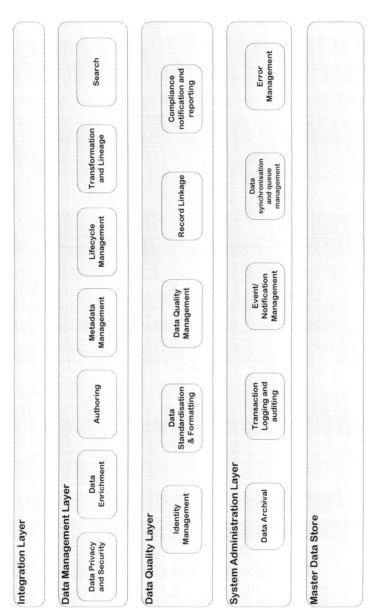

Figure 13 - Component Diagram

Integration Layer

Rather than each component developing separate interfaces to the outside world, it makes sense to have a single interface component that provides an abstraction layer to any underlying MDM service. MDM services are therefore made available through a single interface but have a variety of methods available to use; from one record at a time to bulk access. This component allows us to adopt a loosely coupled approach.

It is illogical to tightly couple our interfaces for ingesting master data and providing access to it with the underlying technology. This would be a fool's errand as we would have to handle many different data sources and technologies and would never get ahead of the curve. The concept of having an integration layer supports this idea. A series of re-useable interfaces or services would be made available that would support a variety of interaction mechanisms. Examples would be:

- Batch service: This is used for large scale export (or import) of master data and should be available as an on demand or scheduled basis.

- Messaging service: This style of service provides single or small volume data exchange using data standards such as XML.

- EII adapter: This provides a service that integrates with Enterprise Information Integration technology.

- Security adapter: Provides the integration with various external security systems/directories that the enterprise may use.

- COTS adapter: This provides a set of interfaces and adapters for common COTS (Commercial of the Shelf) products and external services.

Data Management Layer

Data Privacy and Security

Master data has a high degree of sensitivity around it, both from a data protection and a commercial value perspective and therefore needs to be protected. It wouldn't be appropriate to send customer details that have been flagged as 'not to be contacted by marketing campaigns' to the marketing department for just that use. Any MDM architecture therefore needs to have a comprehensive set of capability in this area.

This subject is discussed further in the next chapter as there is a lot to think about. Not only do we need to manage user access rights as with any system, but also what can and more importantly cannot be done with each piece of data. The two key areas to consider are:

- Data privacy rules; the legal situation in different countries varies based upon the data and what you're going to do with it.

- Data access rules; clearly with the companies valuable data we will need to restrict access to only those people or systems that should have access to it. It doesn't make sense for anyone in the company to have access to the complete customer list or details about new innovative products coming down the line for next year.

Data Enrichment

There is a need for an enrichment component because data typically gets mutated as it journeys around an organisation. For example, you may have specific calculations or name constructs that are commonly used. Rather that perform these rules in each application, it makes sense to perform them in one place, once so as to avoid subtle (but no less troublesome) variations in the rules creeping in. Types of data enrichment cover: data business rules, the management of hierarchies and rules that allow data to be harmonised.

Business Rules

Business rules that are applied to data can become a nightmare to manage if not applied in a central way. For example, if we define that a person's full name is comprised of their first and last name we would have, even with this extremely simplistic example, at least two options on how this can be defined, for example:

- John Smith
- Smith, John

Centrally defining the rules enable simplification of the data management landscape. As we reduce the amount of code and complexity in our various systems we also reduce the cost and risk associated with developing and maintaining such systems.

Hierarchies and Association

We have mentioned that master data is comprised of a number of types one being Enterprise Structure Data; more typically referred to as 'hierarchies'. Hierarchies have special behaviour: they are based on relationships between different nodes (or values) in a tree. There is a need to have a capability to create, and enhance such hierarchies, develop relationships between various pieces of data and the ability to create grouping of specified data based upon aggregation rules so as to simplify the BI world.

Cross Walking

Reference data for the same domain but from different sources will not always be that consistent and therefore we find that a simple one-to-one mapping between different reference lists can be problematic. This is called cross walking and is discussed in detail in chapter 9. The rules used to provide the linkage between different reference lists, need to be managed and the enrichment component would seem the logical place for this.

Authoring Component

A fundamental capability that will need to be performed is the actual authoring of master data. In fact this needs to work against both master data and the meta data we capture to support our master data. It also needs to be able to work against single attributes all the way up to groups and domains of master data. Typical functionality of an authoring component would be:

- CRUD* operations: This allows for the creation, augmentation and deletion of master data.
- Concurrency Management: For the management of check-in and out capability so as to avoid concurrency issues.

For those that don't know, CRUD stands for Create, Read, Update and Delete. It represents the key data operations that are performed to data.

- Version control: Also known as revision control or source control this is the management of changes to the master data values. Each revision is associated with a timestamp and the person making the change so that it can be compared, restored and audited.
- State management: This allows for the master data to go through different levels of approval; for example draft, review, active, inactive and archived.

Metadata Management:

As has been mentioned numerous times, a MDM architecture will contain a wide variety of metadata which is used to describe and manage its master data. This metadata will clearly need to be managed and that in essence is the job of the metadata component.

The type of metadata can include (but is not limited by):

- Matching Attributes: Metadata that identifies attributes that can be used for the purpose of record matching.
- Business rule: Metadata that defines business rules could include aggregation rules, derived attributes etc.
- Exception handling: metadata used to support the exception handling processes such as tolerance levels.
- Default values for attributes.
- Master data schema: The schema is the metadata that describes the logical and physical data models for the various data objects that are held in the MDM hub. This also has the added importance of representing a significant set of company IP or domain knowledge.
- Classification and Taxonomy: The master data will have various classification, typing and taxonomy metadata to support it. This will be particularly

important when searching for specific pieces of master data (see search services).

This component will call upon other components (for example the authoring component).

Lifecycle Management

All data has a lifecycle and associated workflow that defines what happens to it during the course of its life. The Lifecycle management component is responsible for managing those changes in state as the data is initially created, used and eventually deleted/archived.

Transformation and Lineage

This component handles the tracking of data - where it comes from, where it goes to, and how it is transformed. This would cover the identification of the authoritative source and various transformations that occur to the data.

Search Service

There is no point in having master data if no one can find it. This component is responsible for making it easy to find the data you are looking to either understand or use.

There are a number of key features that need to be considered within the scope of this component, namely:

- Search functionality similar to web based search engines.
- Taxonomy based browsing of the master data as this is considered a more effective way of finding things when you don't know the exact name.
- Relationship mappings between master data items.

Data Quality Layer

Identity Management

The identification of master data records is a key capability required by any MDM system. Chapter 10 looks at this subject in more detail but in essence there are two key capabilities required:

- GUID (Global Unique Identifier) & key management
- Identity management

Data Standardisation & Formatting

The conversion of attribute data types to a common standard and the re-formatting of data to that standard is a necessary evil. It would be too complex for each component to have to handle this separately, so we conform all data to a standard set of formats and data types. This ensures consistency and saves a huge effort that would be necessary otherwise.

Data Quality Management

If the data is to be considered as trusted and reliable we need to ensure the quality is high. This component attacks the problem from a number of directions:

- Data validation and cleaning of data: ie checking that data conforms to expected norms and correcting where possible when it doesn't.

- KPI's metrics and measurements: You can't manage something if you're unable to measure the scale of the problem. This sub component will provide various business and technical metrics and KPI's that can be used to drive change. It also provides confidence to data users that the data quality is of significant rigor.

- Reconciliation: Data may be technically validated that it is of the correct format and uses a valid value, but it might not make sense from a wider data perspective. This sub component will harmonise the data with over data sets to allow a reconciled data record to be created.

Record Linkage

One of the key tasks that the MDM solution needs to address is the matching of master data from difference sources into one uniquely identifiable record. This means identifying records from different systems that actually are about the same product or customer and linking them together to create the one true record (or possible the best possible record). The record linkage component is responsible for managing the logic and rules around how this is done. Chapter 11 looks at this in some detail.

Compliance Notification and Reporting

This component is providing two capabilities. Firstly it will notify the appropriate stewards when data policies have been breached. Secondly it will provide a reporting facility to understand compliance across the whole MDM world.

System Administration Layer

This layer contains the various components that provide administrative support to the architecture; such as archiving and audit trails.

Data Archival

Archiving is the practice of storing selected data in a separate storage area that is cheaper so that it can be retrieved later if needed. The process of access the archived data will take far longer than if the data was on-line. Obviously it is only done to data that is not required immediately anymore. In essence we are partitioning the architecture into current master data records and inactive master data records. This requires that an archive storage facility is available.

Clearly not all data is equal and master data archiving needs to take into consideration factors such as how:

- long does this data need to be archived for? Legal and commercial considerations will play a part.
- quickly does this data need to be made available?
- much of this master data do we have to archive, ie the volume.

Transaction Logging and Auditing

It's important to know what's happened to your master data; what processes have been enacted on it, who has accessed it and what has been deleted. We also have the various regulatory compliance challenges that companies in today's world must adhere to. We therefore need to have a capability to notify the organisation of any specific events that have occurred to the data and the current (or previous) state of play.

Regulatory Compliance

Regulatory requirements are putting more strain on stretched compliance operations, as it is increasingly driving the expansion of formal enterprise audit processes to include information technology (IT) assets. In particular, auditors are looking at regulated data residing in databases connected to enterprise applications such as SAP, PeopleSoft, etc. Sarbanes Oxley (SOX), the Health Insurance Portability and Accountability Act (HIPAA) the Payment Card Industry (PCI) standard and other regulatory measures require best practice controls to protect sensitive data. Not only do companies have exposure to fines from regulatory bodies, they also expose themselves to increased reputational risk.

Event/Notification Management

It is important to provide a notification capability, so that other components and external applications know what is going on. Letting the CRM system know that new customer records have just been made available, for example, could be quite important if you expect your CRM system to be kept up to date. This is managed via an event notifier capability that creates the event messages based on the results of internal events. It then publishes the messages to the appropriate consumers.

Data Synchronisation and Queue Management

The various activities and events that are occurring too, or being driven by, the MDM system need to be managed; as they cannot all occur at once due to resource constraints. This means that it is necessary to manage the operations that need to either be scheduled or run on demand.

Error Management

All systems encounter problems that cause errors to occur. This component has the responsibility of gracefully managing those situations and communicating the issue within a controlled way to the system administrators.

Master Data Store

We need a place to store all the master data and this we will call the master data store. The key characteristics of this component are:

- It may be more than one system depending on the nature of the MDM hub style being used (see later in this book). In some instances the master data store may also be a virtual concept rather than a physical database.
- It will handle the storage (physically or virtually) of all four types of master data:
  - Reference data
  - Transaction structure data
  - Enterprise structure data
  - Meta data (both mastered metadata and metadata used to manage the MDM system).
- It has responsibility for archived master data managed. This is via the archiving component but will need a place (or places) to actually store the archived data.

Summary

As we build our MDM capability we need to have an understanding of what we need and why. This chapter provides a reference model for MDM from a purely architectural perspective. It allows us to compare technology, methodologies, different technical and process design options. In essence it gives us a framework within which to architect the future.

5. Master Data is Risky

This chapter addresses an important but generally ignored area which is the management of master data related risk. By this I mean the risk associated with data theft, a breach of data privacy legislation or some other regulatory challenges.

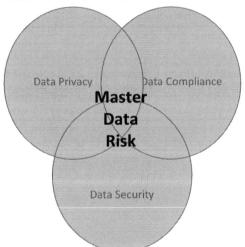

Typically we are talking about 'Enterprise Structure Data' such as customer records but not always. Each data type should be assessed and managed according to its risk profile.

Figure 14 - The intersect of privacy, compliance and security

Data Security

We have already discussed that master data has value and with value comes the need to protect that data from theft or other types of malicious acts.

Identity Theft & Fraud

Identity theft is when your personal details are stolen and identity fraud is when those details are used to commit fraud. Identity theft happens when fraudsters access enough information about someone's identity (such as their name, date of birth, current or previous addresses) to commit identity fraud. Identity theft can take place whether the fraud victim is alive or deceased.

According to the UK Cabinet Office identity fraud costs the UK economy over £1.3 billion annually (claims the BBC's Money programme) and that it is growing at nearly 500%. Fraudsters can use your identity details to do any of the following in your name:

- Open a bank account or take over an existing account.
- Obtain a credit card, loan or apply for state benefit.
- Order goods in your name.
- Obtain a passport or driving licence.

Corporate Data Theft

Theft of data from businesses and public organisations is on the rise and can come in many forms:

- Theft of data by employees: This is typically a disgruntled employee who makes copies of company data to take to a new job or to set up their own businesses. Data theft has become extremely easy as it's possible to copy vast quantities of data within seconds, to cloud-based storage or USB devices.

- Corporate espionage: By this I mean the theft of sensitive data by another company for commercial gain.
- Terrorism or criminal hacking: Cybercrime is on the rise with about 20 attacks on big companies each year; according to law enforcement agencies in the US. The most high profile example of this is the hacking of Target in 2013 to obtain millions of passwords and credit card numbers. This may have been the most successful data breach in U.S. history (at the time).

This list doesn't include everything; for example theft of data by web scraping is often overlooked but can be just as valuable to the thieves.

Layered Security

Based upon the types of risks just discussed it is important that data is secure. The typical approach to this is a layered security model, also known as layered defence. It involves a combining of multiple mitigating security controls. Therefore, in theory, lapses and weaknesses in one defence are made up for with strengths in another.

The term bears some similarity to the military term 'defence in depth' that involves multiple layers of defences. These layers resist rapid penetration by an attacker but yield rather than exhaust themselves hence exhausting the attacker.

The typical layering is:

- Enterprise Boundary: This type of security covers user authentication, authorisation and user rights control.

- Network: This security handles access to the organisations network resources such as drives and printers etc.
- Platform: controls access to the device itself such as a server or a PC.
- Application: this covers authentication, authorisation, encryption
- Data: Data can be protected via encryption, data driven security and/or the complexity of structure (ie meta data driven), SAP is a great example of this as anyone who has worked with it will confirm it can be virtually illegible to the uninitiated.

Data Privacy

Individuals have a right to privacy and this extends to their data. You don't want marketing companies or insurance companies to know your financial or medical details. Data privacy laws vary from country to country, for example within the UK we have the Data Protection Act. The Act says (although not word for word) that if you handle personal information about individuals, you have a number of legal obligations to protect that information. Fundamentally it tells you to use the minimum personal data to satisfy the work you are doing.

The key area of concern in most of these pieces of legislation is around 'Identifiable Data'. This can be defined as any data that can be used to identify an individual such as a person's name or an address and date of birth. The consequences of getting this wrong can vary (depending on the legal jurisdiction) from hefty fines to imprisonment.

Open Data

There are a number of organisations (not for profit, government and commercial) that provide aggregated or anonymised personal data. One such example is the United Kingdom's NHS which has a widely publicised 'Open Data Agenda'. The UK is at the forefront of the open data revolution and since 2010 has made sustained effort to make available patient anonoymised data sets.

The whole field of aggregated personal data is becoming big business and is behind many big data initiatives, where companies are trying to find out patterns in the data. For example by tracking individual patient treatments it becomes possible when you aggregate the results, to discover the effectiveness of different treatments from a quality of life, cost or effectiveness perspective.

Anonymised and Pseudonymised Identifiable Data

One key concept (and challenge) behind such ideas and initiatives is the protection of the individuals identity. This comes in two main forms; anonymised and pseudonymised data.

- Anonymisation: Data anonymisation is where all the identifying attributes of data have been removed and a new encrypted key is used to represent the individual. This process enables the transfer of data between organisations as it reduces the risk of unintended disclosure.
- Pseudonymisation: This is where the most identifying attributes are replaced by one or more artificial identifiers, or pseudonyms. The big difference with this is that if you have the algorithm it is possible to

unscramble the identifiers. The advantage of using pseudonymised identifiers however is that if used across multiple data sets it allows linking of those data records.

Time is a Problem

One area where anonymising/pseudonymising data becomes problematic is time. When we look at data over time we find that it is possible to spot identifiable data. For example let's take an anonymised person with an ID of 1. If we look at data over a 7 year period we might get something like the following:

Figure 15 – Anonymised individual age band changes over time

Anonymised ID	Age Banding	Effective From Date	Effective To Date
1	26-30	1/1/2001	31/12/2001
1	31-35	1/1/2002	31/12/2002
1	31-35	1/1/2003	31/12/2003
1	31-35	1/1/2004	31/12/2004
1	31-35	1/1/2005	31/12/2005
1	31-35	1/1/2006	31/12/2006
1	36-40	1/1/2007	31/12/2007

Whilst every record is completely safe when you look at the records in the context of the wider data set you can identify the following:

- In 2001 he or she was 30, because in 2002 he or she entered the 31-35 age banding.

71

- In 2006 he or she was 35, because in 2007 he or she entered the 36 - 40 age banding. This confirms the first age point and means that the year of birth was 1971. If the data set was more granular (say monthly) we would be able to work out the month and year of birth.

From all this the persons birth year and current age can be worked out. This is now starting to become identifiable and if we mix with other data about the individual it could become only a short step to actually identifying the person.

Data Compliance

Over the last few years there has been a massive growth in the amount of legislation and regulation that impacts on how data is managed. This touches on most industries in one form or another, but has special importance to the financial services and data brokers market, where personally identifiable data is central to their business models. A couple of examples are shown below, but this is a huge and ever changing area that would require a whole book to explain properly.

Basel Accord

In 1988, the Basel Committee on Banking Supervision in Basel, Switzerland, published a set of minimum capital requirements for banks. Later in 1992 the G-10 (Group of Ten) countries enshrined this into law.

Basel I is primarily focused on credit risk and appropriate risk-weighting of assets. It stipulated that banks must have enough funds to cover potential losses. This meant that the total capital should always be more than about 8% of its risk-weighted assets.

Basel 2 replaces the existing standard with a framework that seeks to providing a more risk-sensitive, flexible, but more heavily regulated, approach. The three essential requirements of Basel II are:

- Mandating that capital allocations are risk sensitive.
- Separating credit risks from operational risks and quantifying both.
- Reducing the scope or possibility of regulatory arbitrage, by attempting to align the real or economic risk precisely with regulatory assessment.

The requirements to calculate Risk Weighted Assets (RWA) and associated capital, span two broad categories of data - transaction data and master data.

In this context master data describes such data as obligors, business units, legal vehicles, products, asset classes, securities data, corporate action events, market quotes of prices and exchange rates. To allocate data into their appropriate asset classes or risk buckets we need reliable master data. Therefore master data becomes pivotal in fulfilling Basel risk analysis. History has shown that inaccurate reports lead to stress test failures, a rise in regulatory complaints and worse - banks not getting a handle on its credit risks and becoming prime targets for takeover.

Sarbanes-Oxley (SOX)

The Sarbanes–Oxley Act of 2002 is a US federal law that sets standards for all U.S. public company boards, management and public accounting firms. Within this Act are defined reporting and compliance requirements. Master data is seen as integral to these requirements just as with the Basel Accord.

Risk Management

Risk management is about identifying, understanding and co-ordinating resources to minimise or remove the impact of the risk. Often with master data there is not enough co-ordination across the organisation on data risk. In this section we will identify the types of risk that need managing.

Operational Risk

This risk is that the data will be lost, stolen or corrupted in some way. Having no access to customer data or data about orders would be quite catastrophic. Stolen data has a number of consequences, not only loss of business due to competitors using the stolen data against you but also compliance risks (see below).

Reputational Risk

Reputational risk is all about a threat or danger to the good name or standing of an organisation. This can occur via a number of routes:

- directly as the result of the actions of the company itself.
- indirectly due to the actions of an employee or employees.
- tangentially through other peripheral parties such as joint venture partners or suppliers.

Reputational risk is a hidden danger that can pose a threat to the survival of the biggest and best-run companies. It can often wipe out millions or billions of dollars in market capitalisation or lost revenues, and can occasionally result in a change at the uppermost levels of management. The biggest problem with reputational risk is that it can literally erupt out of nowhere. In some instances, reputational risk can be mitigated through prompt damage control measures, which is essential in this age of instant communication and social media networks. In other instances, this risk can be more insidious and last for years. As an example this can be caused by data privacy breaches if customer data security is of concern to the market.

Strategic Risk

This is the risk associated with losses that might occur due to the pursuit of an unsuccessful business plan. This type of loss can be catastrophic in nature. It can arise due to a number of reasons which include: making poor business decisions, substandard execution of decisions, inadequate resource allocation and failure to respond well to changes in the business environment.

Last, but not least, business plans can go wrong due to incorrect data being used originally to build the plan or business case. This is clearly something that MDM can impact directly, as has been indicated through the earlier chapters of this book.

Compliance (Legal) Risk

Compliance risk is the current and prospective risk to earnings or capital that arises from the violation of laws, rules, regulations, prescribed practices, internal policies, procedures, or ethical standards. It can also occur where the laws, or rules, governing certain products, or activities, may be ambiguous or untested.

Falling foul of compliance risk exposes the organisation to financial penalties, damages, and the possible voiding of contracts. It also can have the subtle impact of diminishing reputation, reducing franchise value, limiting business opportunities, reducing expansion potential, and an inability to enforce contracts.

Summary

Master data has risks associated with it that need to be understood and managed. It is also important to understand that there are a number of challenges that come with understanding that risk, namely:

- Determining real cost benefit is tough as it's often based on the assumption that risk is likely to occur. Some of the risks may only occur once in a decade.
- As the technology landscape is constantly changing, risks therefore need to be re-assessed in line with these changes.
- Regulations are not necessarily globally implemented so each jurisdiction may have different laws or nuances to the same law.
- It is important to measure the governance process and risk assessments are part of that.

6. Magnum Opus

"Hence they are mistaken who strive to elicit the medicine for the tinging of metals from animals or vegetables. The tincture and the metal tinged must belong to the same root or genus; and as it is the imperfect metals upon which the Philosopher's Stone is to be projected, it follows that the powder of the Stone must be essentially Mercury. The Stone is the metallic matter which changes the forms of imperfect metals into gold, as we may learn from the first chapter of 'The Code of Truth': 'The Philosophical Stone is the metallic matter converting the substances and forms of imperfect metals'; and all Sages agree that it can have this effect only by being like them."

The Stone of the Philosophers by Edward Kelly, Note 2 [4].

The philosopher's stone is a legendary substance said to be able to turn lead (or other base metals) into gold. It was meant to represent the greatest achievement of western alchemy. The journey that the alchemist went through to discover the philosopher's stone was known as the Magnum Opus, from the Latin for 'Great Work'.

In the world of Master Data the Great Work, or Magnum Opus, is the creation of the Golden Source. In this chapter we look at two foundational concepts; the 'Golden Source' and the

'Authoritative Source'. These ideas between then address two fundamental questions:

- Where does my data come from?
- How do I know it is correct?

Golden Source

One of the common approaches to MDM is to pull together the organisations master data into a single system. A database where all the consuming applications of the enterprise can go to get there Master Data. This is called the Golden Source or sometimes it is referred to as the "Golden Copy". This approach is the basis of the Master Data hub architecture which we discuss later in this book and often is used, as a term, interchangeable with the Master Data Hub. There are a number of different approaches to this, but in essence they will all bring the data together; either physically or virtually.

The golden source concept is foundational to MDM as it is a core idea behind concepts of single customer view or single product view. We take this approach because if the resolution of all the various data integration issues is resolved once for each record rather than multiple times (ie once for every system) we have a massive efficiency saving and an opportunity to improve quality.

The principles underlying the golden source are:

- Principle 1 - It is made up of one or more datasets: It is typical that a master data record (especially key business ones such as customer) will be composites of multiple pieces of data from multiple systems.

- Principle 2 - It must be trust worthy: By this I mean the golden source must be based upon data sets that have authority (see later in this chapter). So therefore it follows that the golden source needs to be accurate, complete and known. By known I mean that we have clarity in understanding its lineage.
- Principle 3 - It must not be duplicated: There is no point having a couple of places within the golden source system to get the same piece of data. This just leads to confusion and doubt about which one is correct. This is obviously on top of the overhead of managing a piece of data more than once.
- Principle 4 - It is (often) not the original record as the golden source is not normally managed by the system that actually created/authored the original piece of data.

A golden source is therefore made up of many golden records which can be thought of as the most valid version of the records possible, from all the constituent data sets that are required to make them.

The golden source concept is foundational to MDM as it is a core idea behind concepts of single customer view or single product view.

Authoritative Sources

For the golden source concept to work the data must be trusted. Clearly our golden source will not get much traction if it is not using the correct set of data. We achieve this by identifying and sourcing our data from the one true authoring system. This is called in MDM terms the authoritative source.

The authoritative source is the system that actually creates the data in the first place

---

The authoritative source is the system that actually creates the data in the first place. It is important to know where the data came from so as to be able to remove the degradation that can occur as data travels from system to system. It's a bit like a game of Chinese whispers, the further away from the original source we can get the more changes and miss understandings that occur to the data. For example a CRM system may capture a customer's date of birth as a full date. This data is passed to another system which stored the date of birth as a year and month only. This is in turn passed onto a third system which takes this year and month of birth and converts it to a date of birth again but because this third system has no knowledge of the original system that captures the data it creates a default date for the customer of the first of the month. That means that our customer with a birth date of 13th July 1975 ends up with a birth date of 1st July 1975.

Figure 16 - Transformation of a date

Also known as the 'Book of Record', authoritative sources can be outside your organisation. For example it is common place to use the ISO list of countries (ISO 3166) rather than create your own list. ISO 3166 has as its purpose the establishment of a set of internationally recognisable codes for countries (to be completely correct this does also include territories and geographical areas or interest). The standard doesn't in fact define the name of the country; this is sourced from the United Nations. Changes are added automatically when published by the United Nations. Not meaning to blow the trumpet of the ISO but this particular standard is used widely in my experience. Why would you create your own list, or manage an internal country list, with all the effort involved in managing such a list when it is available pre managed? The only prohibitive factor becomes the price of buying verses the price of managing.

Identifying the Authoritative Source

Originating sources of master data may not be as easy to find as may at first seem the case. The authoritative source may be hidden behind some complex patterns that you will need to understand to find it. In some situations the particular master data will all come from the same source but this is not as common as you would expect. There are in general four other scenario's you will need to consider when searching for the authoritative source of your master data:

- Subset of Columns
- Subset of Records
- Subset of Columns within a subset of records
- Shadow Systems

Subset of Columns

A subset of the attributes that make up your master data record can be found in one system and the other attributes can be found in a second, third or fourth system. For example our master data maybe for a product; we get the name and description of the product with its brand details from a product marketing system and the price from our accountancy system.

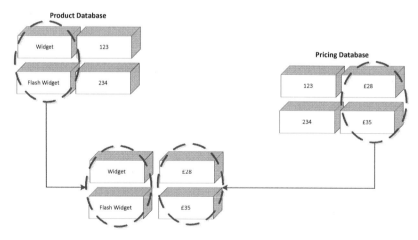

Figure 17 - Subset of columns

As you can see from figure 17, these attributes are pulled together to make a contiguous record of product data.

Subset of Records

Not all the records can be found in a single source. For example taking the product example from above, we may have our luxury products coming from one system and the economy products coming from a second system.

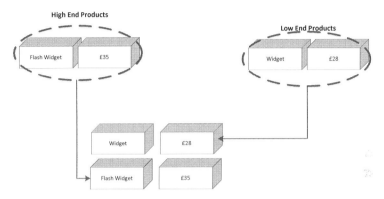

Figure 18 - Subset of records

Subset of Columns within a Subset of Records

This category represents a mixture of the previous two. We have some attributes coming from the luxury product system that are used just for the luxury product records. A similar situation exists for the economy product data but all product records get the price attribute from the same source.

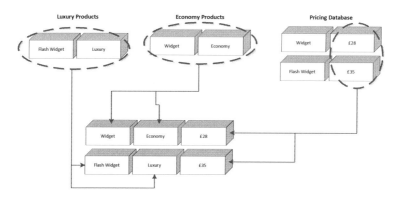

Figure 19 - Sourcing the golden record

This is clearly a more complex situation but quite common (and I suspect my example is a bit simple in comparison to the real world).

Shadow Systems

One complication sometimes experienced is the shadow system. This is a human based system that copies the data from the real authoring system via a human being into a second system which then looks as though it has created the original master data. These situations are notoriously hard to spot and with the rise of local databases and spreadsheets are all too common.

Summary

In this chapter we have identified and explored two foundational concepts behind MDM; the authoritative source and the golden source. They mean the following:

- The authoritative source is the system that actually creates the data in the first place.
- The golden source (or record) is a harmonised data set that we can use that is derived from the authoritative sources.

These ideas whilst quite simple to understand are filled with challenges within the real world but are worth the pain of getting right.

7. It's a Huge Job

The master data landscape is huge, vast and expansive; even though it is only a subset of all the data in an organisation. Just imagine for a moment the effort involved in mapping and fully documenting it. There are probably not enough hours in the day and enough people in the organisation to do this job, let alone keeping it updated. You will never have enough manpower to map the whole master data landscape. Even if you did have the resources as soon as you're finished it is likely to be out of date.

This chapter looks at addresses the questions of what master data do we have and where does it really come from. It applies a pragmatic approach that should enable you to stand a chance of reaching a high degree of completeness.

How much Master Data is there?

Before we address the question of what do we have and where does it come from, it is important to put this problem into context. Organisations are creating and storing vast amounts of data, year after year. This is an ever increasing problem with the amount of data in the world doubling each year. It is estimated that by 2011 we had 1.8 zettabytes of data and by 2020 the world will generate 50 times this amount of data. [5]

So how much data does a typical organisation actually have? Let's look at two examples:

Our first example is a local government organisation for a city, or possibly a state (in the UK we call these counties). Our local government body probably has a budget of about £350 million per year, and would likely have at least 10 different key database applications for areas such as HR, accounts, social care issues and planning.

In addition to these key systems there is the shadow IT world. There are a multitude of satellite systems sitting on peoples desks, or used by small teams but not probably known or managed by any central IT function. Let's assume for the purposes of this example that there are only 20 of them.

Based upon the above example we can make a few assumptions, which we can use to give a sense of the volume of data attributes we are faced with. If we assume the following:

- each table within a database on average has 20 attributes.
- each main system has 25 tables
- each satellite system has 10 tables (or spreadsheets which we can treat as equivalent)

Multiplying out the numbers means we get the following (as shown in the table below):

Main Systems	Main Systems	Satellite Systems
No of Database systems	10	20
No of Tables	50	10
No of Attributes	20	20
Total number of Attributes	10,000 (10*50*20)	4,000 (20*10*20)
The grand total	14,000 attributes	

Figure 20 - The number of attributes for a local government organisation

Our second example is a large multinational corporation. If we make the assumption that:

- it's database tables are of a similar size.
- the number of systems is different, let's say 25 key systems and 100 satellite.
- the complexity of the key systems is higher, let's say 100 tables.

So using these numbers we get the results shown in the table below.

Main Systems	Main Systems	Satellite Systems
No of Database systems	25	100
No of Tables	100	10
No of Attributes	20	20

Total number of Attributes	50,000 (25*100*20)	20,000 (10*10*20)
The grand total	70,000 attributes	

Figure 21 - The number of attributes for a large company

Based on these two sets of numbers, we can now ask the question how much data is likely to be master data. Without going into the specifics let's assume only 10% of our data can be classified as Master Data. In reality the number is likely to be far higher. This means that we get the 7,000 attributes for the large corporate and 1,400 attributes for the government body to worry about. Quite a lot I think?

So just think for a moment how big is your own organisations master data landscape.

Where is all our Master Data?

Now we have a general appreciation of how much master data there is likely to be we need to find it all! So how do we accomplish this without an army of people? The answer is by small baby steps through an evolving process. The steps we need to go through are:

1. What Master Data do we have
2. Identify the key applications we need to worry about.
3. Map the applications to the underlying database systems that store all the data.
4. Map the master data to database
5. Map the master data to tables

6. Complete a CRUD analysis to validate where the data is authored.

The rest of this chapter will work through this process and provide some ideas and guidance on how to accomplish each step.

Step 1- What Master Data do we have?

To understand what master data we have, we need to understand the wider set of data used across the enterprise. The best way to understand this is via an 'Enterprise Data Model' or EDM. This is basically a consolidated understanding of the companies' enterprise level data and by definition will encompass the enterprises master data.

The Enterprise Data Model

It is also important to clarify what is meant by the term 'Enterprise Data Model'. In its simplistic form, an enterprise data model differs from an individual project based data model on two accounts

- Firstly, it is at a higher level of abstraction as it doesn't go below a logical level.
- Secondly, it has a wider scope of coverage as it provides an integrated view of the data across the entire organisation.

If we take as an example the definition of a customer data entity, we may have a collection of key attributes (name, address, etc) which are used by many different systems. Through an Enterprise Data Model we are able to provide a common standard in terms of definition.

The model takes the perspective of the whole organisation (or enterprise) and therefore the types of issues it addresses are at that level, for example the:

- Promotion of commonality, in terms of definition, across the various database applications.

- Reduction of risks associated with technology projects by providing organisational best practice for data.

- Improvement of the quality of data and associated business processes.

From the enterprise data model it should be possible based upon our definition of master data types to identify most if not all the master data we need to worry about.

To know more about the Enterprise Data Model please see my previous book on this subject ('The Enterprise Data Model: A framework for enterprise data architecture', ISBN: 0956582915)

Step 2 – Identify Key Application

Next we need an inventory of applications and associated database systems. Obviously this will need to be tempered with a level of pragmatism and therefore typically you will only look at the key systems. If time permits it would add extra value to go as far as possible with this. We distinguish between applications and databases because not all applications have a database and not all databases actually have an application using them directly.

Step 3 – Map Application to Database

Map the applications to the underlying database systems that store all the data.

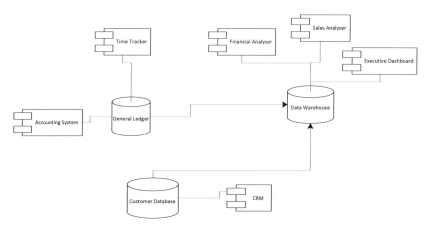

Figure 22 - an example of application to database

	Customer Database	General Ledger	Data Warehouse
Accounting System		✓	
Time Tracker		✓	
Financial Analyser			✓
Sales Analyser			✓
Executive Dashboard			✓
CRM	✓		

Figure 23 - Application to database matrix

The example above is for an imaginary company that sells widgets. It has three databases, and five applications that use those databases. If we were to map out the application to database matrix we get the table just below it (figure 23). It should be noted that we can have applications that draw data from multiple databases and also databases that only connect to other databases and have no applications associated with them at all.

Step 4 - Map the Master Data to Database

Now that we understand what data is important to the organisation (as identified by our enterprise data model) and we know where all (or at least most) of our data is stored we can start to piece this together.

Taking the conceptual level version of the enterprise data model proceed to map each conceptual level data entity to each database that stores this type of data. Obviously if time allows you can perform this activity at a logical level as well but for pragmatic reasons I would expect that a conceptual level will do in the first instance.

With our example company we have the following conceptual data entities:

- Product
- Customer
- Sales

We shall ignore Sales data as although identified in our enterprise data model, it is not in fact master data and should be excluded from this analysis. As you drill down to a more logical level you will find that there is likely to be master data hidden in it but that will complicate matters too much in our initial stages of analysis. As can be seen from the table below, customer can be found in all three databases whilst product is only in the general ledger and the data warehouse.

	Customer Database	General Ledger	Data Warehouse
CUSTOMER	✓	✓	✓
PRODUCT		✓	✓

Figure 24 - Data Entity to database matrix

Step 5 - Mapping Tables to Master Data Entities

We have identified that we have only two key master data conceptual entities 'Product' and 'Customer'. We know which systems use this master data (at least at a high level), so now let's look at this down another level of detail. It should be noted that this stage is optional and will probably be an activity that would be done over time as a background activity.

If we take customer we can now look within each system, and understand the interpretation of customer master data that exists there. Within the general ledger database we find that there are the following tables that contain customer related data:

- Address (TBL_ADDRESS)
- Customer (TBL_CUSTOMER)
- Account (TBL_ACCOUNT)

Within the customer database we have these tables:

- Customer (CRM_CUST)
- Address (CRM_ADDRSS)
- Family Relationships (CRM_RELATION)

So if we map this information to our conceptual level enterprise data model entities we get something like this:

Database	Table	Enterprise Entity	
		Logical level	Conceptual level
General Ledger	TBL_ADDRESS	Party Address	Customer
General Ledger	TBL_CUSTOMER	Party	Customer
General Ledger	TBL_ACCOUNT	Account	Customer
Customer Database	CRM_CUST	Party	Customer
Customer Database	CRM_ADDRSS	Party Address	Customer
Customer Database	CRM_RELATION	Party Relationship	Customer

Figure 25 - Tables to master data entities

Step 6 - Complete a CRUD Analysis

Analysis of each database system (and its associated applications) will give us an understanding of the states that data can be in within these systems. The valid states we need to contend with are: Create, Read, Update and Delete or CRUD for short. We can now map these entities to each database using the CRUD notation as follows:

	Customer DB	General Ledger	Data Warehouse
Product	R	CRUD	RD
Customer	CRUD	CRUD	RD

Figure 26 - Simple CRUD example

With our relatively simple example we can already see a few interesting facts:

95

- Firstly the data warehouse doesn't create or update any Product or Customer data. This means the only two databases we are interested in are the general ledger and the customer database. (It should be noted that the data warehouse will delete data as it only holds a rolling 5 years.)
- Customer data is created, updated and deleted in both the general ledger and customer database. This is very dangerous. It is possible that if would look into the detail we will find that actually only some of the master data is authored in the customer database and the same with the general ledger.
- Product data is created, updated and deleted by the financial department via the general ledger.

What next

Now that we have a set of information about how our master data is created and flows through the organisation it is important to not let it go stale. It should be considered an ongoing task to keep this information up to date and relevant. There are three strategies to adopt to make this happen which, in no particular order, are:

- Repository: The results should be stored in a repository system so that they can be accessed and maintained as required by the organisation. Don't use a spreadsheet as it will just get lost, duplicated and maintained in silo's.
- Governance: This needs to become part of our governance BAU (business as usual) processes. Our business and technical processes around data governance need to have the maintenance and creation of this information instilled into them. For example any

new system should map all its data to the enterprise data model as part of the design activity.

- Education: Organisational buy in is as always an important factor toward success. You must make sure the individuals responsible for this information understand why we are capturing it and how it is to be used.

If the organisation is to large or the problem space to complex start small. Define a BAU governance process (as outlined above) and gradually build up this knowledge over time.

The sad thing about this type of analysis is that it is rarely ever done at the enterprise level. Typically it is undertaken at a departmental level. By following these approaches you are more likely to achieve success.

Summary

We have now looked at an approach for identifying our authoritative sources. Our 6 step process provides a way of providing the initial mapping and future refinements of that mapping. We have also looked at how much master data we are likely to be faced with. This will help in managing expectations and resources when working through this process. We have also addressed the issue of maintaining our new found understanding of our real authoritative data sources.

8. The Hub

Master data is typically found scattered throughout the enterprise. It will therefore exist in an inconsistent and incomplete form with suboptimal quality levels. A MDM system needs to resolve this by merge it all together, fix any issues and then finally distribute it to the various applications, in a heterogeneous environment, that need it.

The predominant approach to MDM in today's world is called the 'Hub Architecture'. It has gained this name because, as the name suggests, the approach is to have a central point where all master data passes through prior to reaching its destination; just like an airport or railway hub. The analogy goes further than that. Dictionary.com define 'Hub' as 'a centre around which other things revolve or from which they radiate; a focus of activity, authority, commerce, transportation, etc'. The MDM Hub architecture is the focus of master data activity within the organisation and provides us with the authoritative, golden source of master data.

As with airports, a Hub architecture is complex and challenging and over time a number of different versions of this architecture have arisen. The list of versions varies depending on who you speak too, or who's books and articles you read, but as far as I can ascertain the list is as follows:

- Virtual
- Registry
- Consolidation
- Reconciliation
- Transaction

The names above are a mixture of my own and industry recognised terminology. Over the course of the next few sections we will explore what the differences are between each type.

Virtual Style

As its name suggests the virtual style of MDM (also known as the 'External Reference Style) is a bit of an illusion. It doesn't really do very much except re-direct you request for master data directly to the authoritative source of this data. This re-direct can be as simple as a business process that defines where data is to be sourced from, to a software solution that will manage the re-direct request for you.

The example spreadsheet table, shown below, could be considered a virtual MDM hub as it provides the re-direction details. A single database view (or a number of them) could likewise also be considered as one.

Data Entity	Attributes	Owning System	SQL Statement
Customer	Name, Income Banding, Shipping Address	Sales System	Select Name, Income, Address From CUSTOMER

Figure 27 - Virtual Hub example

This style of MDM hub is rarely written about or even mentioned in the marketplace. The cynic in me puts this down to the following reasons:

- A virtual MDM hub doesn't require a sophisticated software product.
- Because of this it is of little interest to the various MDM software vendors or consultancies, as there is no money in it for them.
- Due to this lack of interest little marketing spend is targeted in this area hence little is written about it.

Pro's	Con's
1/ Quick and cheap to implement as there is not really that much too it.	1/ Slow performance as you have to pass through to the authoritative source of data.
2/ Its low risk as the likelihood of project problems are low; due to the low tech nature of this approach.	2/ It doesn't improve data quality and can't handle complex very well; as some records will be comprised of data from multiple systems.
4/ It also has the added advantage that it annoys the hell out of the MDM industry.	

Registry Style

The Registry style of hub holds identifiers for all of the master data, data sourcing details as well as attributes used for matching purposes (such as the email address, postal address and telephone number). These extra details allow the hub to find the customer record you're interested in even if you don't have the Customer ID.

The hub will not fix, change or alter in anyway the source data but instead will assume that the data is correct and just re-direct your request to the source system.

When a request to get a composite view of a data entity is received by the hub, it has to build the view using the cross-reference data and the global data entity ID. In essence this style creates a read only, non-harmonised, single and consistent access point for all master data. On its own it can be a massive step forward.

Pro's	Con's
1/ This option is also relatively quick and cheap to implement. Of the more traditional MDM approaches it is the cheapest. 2/ Also the most low risk of the traditional MDM approaches. 3/ Handles some of the complexity.	1/ Slow performance as you have to pass through to the authoritative source of data. 2/ Doesn't improve data quality or harmonise the data leaving the consuming application with all the oddities between systems to handle.

Consolidation Style

The consolidation style of MDM hub does exactly what its name suggests; it consolidates all the master data into one place for ease of consumption by downstream systems. The data is still owned by the authoring system. Instead of the hub having to hunt around all the databases in real time, and pull the data together, it is pre-processed and pulled together by the MDM hub into a single repository. This is really just an extension of the Registry style except all the data is held and there is no need to go back to the source each time to build the record on the fly. This is sometimes referred to as a reference data or master data warehouse.

Pro's	Con's
1/ This style of hub will assign unique global identifiers to the matched records and provide harmonisation of the data (within reason).	1/ Doesn't improve data quality.
	2/ Requires a lot of pre-processing so timeslots will need to be made available for this.
2/ Performance is great as all the data is available pre-processed.	3/ The data will not be completely up to date as a time lag will exist.
3/ Typically used within the data warehousing world as it replaces a lot of the work that ETL would be doing in prepping the data for the warehouse.	

Reconciliation Style

The reconciliation style is similar to the consolidation style except rather than just consolidating the data it looks at resolving data issues. Data from across the organisation is sucked in and then cleansing & matching routines are run.

The problem with this approach though is that the correct data is never sent back, which to me seems senseless. All this achieves is an illusion of improved data quality but the data is still bad and will only get worse; because the source systems aren't aware or don't feel they need to address the problem. It's a bit like having an illness that leaves marks on your face and rather than paying a visit to your doctor, to get an appropriate treatment, you just apply makeup to hide the effects.

Pro's	Con's
1/ All the benefits of the consolidation style: • Unique identifiers • Performance • Data Warehousing ETL 2/ Will provide better quality data downstream.	1/ Data quality problems within source system never get any better. 2/ Requires a lot of pre-processing so timeslots will need to be made available for this. 3/ The data will not be completely up to date as a time lag will exist.

Transaction Style Architecture

At the extreme end of MDM we have the transaction style of hub architecture. With this style, the hub itself becomes the authoritative source of master data. The source systems publish its data and the MDM hub stores this master data, matches it and fixes any issues. After the collection and enhancing of the data has occurred the Transaction Hub would publish the master data back to the originating system. This means that these enriched data records now replace the original master data from the source systems. In effect the Hub becomes the place that master data is maintained and enhanced rather than the original source systems.

The aim of this style of Hub architecture is that master data (where ever it may exist) is consistent, accurate and complete at all times. We find that read and write operations on master data are done through the MDM System. Any applications that need to change a piece of master data invoke the MDM services offered by the MDM System to make that change. This results in consistency of the master data. In essence the hub has become the authoritative source of master data as in effect it is generating the actual valid records. Deploying an MDM solution with this style will require deep intrusion into the application systems; intercepting business transactions in such a way that they interact with the MDM System for master data changes, or the deployment of global transaction mechanism such as a two-phase commit infrastructure.

Pro's	Con's
1/ The master data quality is significantly improved.	1/ The cost of deploying this style is extremely high. All attributes of the master data model need to be harmonised and cleansed before loaded into the MDM System, this makes the master data integration phase more costly.
2/ The access is usually quicker because there is no need for federation anymore.	
3/ Workflows for collaborative authoring of master data can be deployed much easier.	2/ The synchronisation between the MDM System and application systems is not free.
4/ Reporting on master data is easier now that all master data attributes are in a single place.	

A variant of the transaction style MDM hub is the Coexistence style in which the authoring of master data can happen in the MDM System as well as in the application systems. This approach creates a delay between the place where the change is made and its synchronisation across the rest of the MDM architecture, i.e. data consistency is pending. The smaller the window of propagation, the more this implementation style moves towards absolute consistency of data and in effect the transaction style of hub.

One Size Doesn't Fit All

Alas as is typical of IT one size of solution doesn't fit all problems. In fact we now have a number of evolutionary styles. By this I mean that an organisation can start with one style and evolve onto a second or a third as the business requirements change overtime.

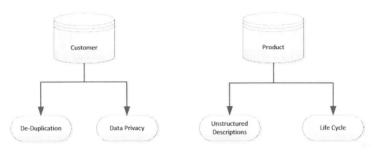

Figure 28 - One sizes doesn't fit all

It is also the case that within the same solution multiple styles maybe required; different types of master data require to be managed in different ways. This may be due to the value or importance of the data or because it just has distinctly different needs.

Customer data, for example, often suffers from multiple versions of the true and will potentially require resolution to create a true and valid customer record. Also you might have to deal with data privacy legislation.

On the other hand product data may be far more static and possible sourced from a single product system for different phases of its life. Also you may have to content with the vast amount of unstructured data such as product brochures and specification fact sheets. This in essence represents an additional dimension to the properties and behaviours of master data.

Reference Data Management

Whilst looking at the subject of hub architectures it makes sense to mention Reference Data Management (RDM) systems. These are a sub set of the MDM world that is focused on managing reference data specifically.

Before looking at RDM systems it is worth taking a few moments to reflect on what we have already explored about reference data. In chapter 2 we explored master data and the types of data that make it up. We divided master data into four distinct classifications:

- Reference Data
- Transaction Structure Data
- Enterprise Structure Data
- Enterprise Metadata

We described reference data as data that is used to categorise other data within systems. This type of data is also known as: Lookup Data, Domain Values or just Codes and Descriptions. We also defined a set of characteristics that are specific to reference data, these are:

- It only has a few rows and columns so it only needs a small amount of storage.
- It is not normally covered by data privacy legislation or commercial sensitivity.
- In some cases it can be re-created quite easily. An example would be the ISO country list which can be just reloaded from source.
- Sometimes the origins of this data can be external.
- It is simple in structure. A simple domain database structure may be enough to store all this type of data.
- It can be challenging to link across different reference systems for the same thing.

- It is very slowly changing. Reference data changes relatively infrequently, but it does change over time, and given its ubiquity, synchronizing reference data values and managing changes across the enterprise is a major challenge.

Reference Data Pains

Managing reference data can be a painful experience. We can take the data challenges in the healthcare industry as a case in point. Healthcare is a complex industry with doctors, hospitals, plan providers and insurance companies working together to provide an effective service to patients, whilst ensuring payments and bills are processed.

As part of the communication to government and governing bodies and between the healthcare professionals, diagnosis and clinical procedures are classified using systems such as ICD9 and ICD10. The transition from ICD-9 to ICD-10 has an impact on processes and IT systems as the two coding systems work at quite different levels of granularity.

Data analysis to understand utilisation, quality of treatment etc will possible require cross walking between the two different classification systems depending on the time horizons used in the analysis. Cross walking is discussed in chapter 9 but is a good example of the problems caused by reference data.

Reference Data Management Systems

The proliferation of systems across the enterprise will, unless controlled, typically define their own sets of reference data. This is compounded by a lack of standardisation of reference data standards.

All this hassle would vanish if we defined a single source of the truth for reference data. This brings us straight back to the MDM argument. In reality whether you have a separate RDMS to your MDM system, or combine them, they are extremely similar. It should be noted that the technology used for MDM, will be normally of a magnitude more sophisticated than that used for purely reference data.

Summary

In this chapter we have looked at the MDM Hub. This is a central concept and has many different styles and flavours:

- Virtual style refers to a simple re-direction mechanism.
- Registry style is an intelligent re-direction mechanism that understands what records it's looking for.
- Consolidation style is more aimed at data warehousing problems and basically pulls all the master data together physically.
- Reconciliation style hides the issues with the data by fixing them within the hub so that consuming systems do not need to manage the various data problems that exist.
- Transaction style is the full Monty approach to MDM where the hub starts to be where the master data is managed rather than the original authoring system.

It is important when creating the MDM hub not to be driven by the technology but instead by the needs of the organisation and the data. We have also seen how it is possible that more than one style can co-exist within a single architecture.

9. The Cross Walk

This chapter is dedicated to one category of master data – reference data - and one of its specific nuances – the cross walk! Reference data is created to serve the needs of a particular group of users, or systems, to categorise other data. Typically when we mix reference data together from different sources, we unfortunately find that a simple one-to-one mapping of values (or harmonisation) is rare. Although the reference data may be about the same subject, different approaches and methodologies will be behind its creation. The process of mapping one reference standard to another is called cross-walking.

Cross walking is a major headache when undertaking any kind of data integration project. It is even more of a problem for MDM projects; as the guilty reference values will need to be potentially available across large parts of the organisation.

Collision Points

When harmonising reference data values from different standards, there are a number of collision points in the merging that may occur. This section looks at the key ones.

Definition Matching

A value in one reference set may not find a directly comparable value in the other reference set; because the definition or semantics are different, even if only subtlety.

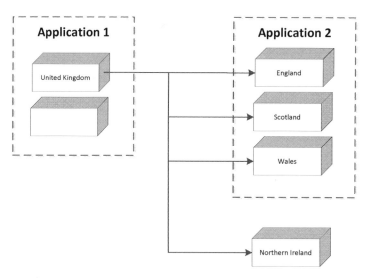

Figure 29 - Country crosswalk

As an example let's assume we have two systems (with the highly imaginative names of Application 1 and Application 2), each with a lookup reference list of countries. Application 1 has the United Kingdom as a country whilst Application 2 has England, Scotland and Wales. The United Kingdom is actually made up of England, Scotland, Wales and Northern Ireland so we have a difference in meaning between the two. This means that in reality the definition of our two country lists are slightly different and cannot be considered as equivalent. Before people write into me explaining that I have miss defined the United Kingdom, in an effort to keep this example simple I have ignored Crown dependencies (Guernsey, Jersey and the Isle of Man) and the British Overseas Territories.

Many-to-One Matching

One reference set uses only one attribute to define its reference list, whilst the other reference set uses two or possible three attributes to define its reference set.

The process of mapping one reference standard to another is called cross-walking.

Let us use a marketing company example to explain this problem. Our imaginary company has both a UK and US operation. In the UK they have a concept of brand; which is based upon a discrete list of available brands as shown in the table below.

Figure 30 - List of UK Brand's

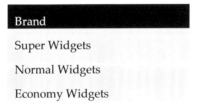

Brand
Super Widgets
Normal Widgets
Economy Widgets

In the US though we have a different definition for brand. The definition is made up of two elements; a brand family and a brand name. These two elements are combined together to form the equivalent of the UK brand.

Figure 31 - List of US Brands

Brand Family	Brand Name
Hot Rod	Red
Hot Rod	Blue
Hot Rod	Silver
Special	Gold
Special	Black

Furthermore, one standard may contain extra elements and descriptors that cannot even be paired with the other system. Using the above example, Hot Rod Silver may not easily map onto the UK brands.

Consistency Matching

Consistency in how data was originally entered is important. It is a common issue that elements from two different reference sources semantically match but the rules defining how data is entered may differ radically. Examples of this would be:

- data types; in one system the attribute is defined as text whilst in another it is defined as a number. This type of cross-walking can best be handled by a conversion or reformatting of the data.

- ranges of values; the age banding in one system is 31 to 40 whilst the second system has an age banding of 30 to 39.

- mandatory or optional usage of the element when entering values; in system one the value is mandatory whilst the same value in a second system is optional.

This becomes challenging when we have to decide what to do with the optional values.

Matching Single vs. Multiple or Compound Data Objects

A special type of data object that can cause added problems is the multiple, or compound, data object. Many database systems allow the relationships between several data records or media items to be expressed. For example, a video program might have a transcript (text document), brochure (pdf), DVD (non-digital medium for order fulfilment), and other items associated with it. If an end user searches for the video program, the search results report the related media items as well. These associated or related items are often housed as a "multiple" or "compound" data object. Many databases actually refer to them as "container fields." If the source and target metadata system use different methods to identify and report multiple or compound objects, then a mismatch in mapping occurs.

Single and Two Dimensional Arrays

Another data type (I use this term loosely) is the single or two dimensional array. An array is a composite variable that can store data values of different types.

Matching Hierarchical and Flat Metadata Standards

Some metadata standards, like IEEE-LOM (Learning Object Metadata) use a very hierarchical structure to organise the relationships between metadata elements. These relationships can often become quite complex. PBCore v1.1 uses a hierarchical set of element interdependencies. Other standards, such as Dublin Core, are flat in nature, with no implied or expressed hierarchy. Trying to pair metadata elements from a hierarchical and a flat system can be troublesome.

History

One last point before we move onto the approaches to addressing the crosswalk challenge. Maintaining the mapping between different reference lists has a historical element to it as well. Over time standards change and evolve. It therefore becomes necessary to keep the mapping up-to-date; otherwise the linkage will becomes outdated and eventually useless. The implication of this is that there is a need to sustain a historical perspective and ongoing expertise in each standard.

Managing the Crosswalk

So how do you handle the crosswalk problem? There are a number of strategies that when combined together provide a way through this quagmire. My 5 point plan is as follows:

1. Business Rules
2. Industry Standards
3. SME Expertise
4. The Enterprise Data Model
5. Data Governance

Business Rules

The first strategy is to develop a series of business rules that allow these differing reference sets to be matched. Clearly these rules will be based upon SME experience, best fit and compromise. It is important to harness this set of rules so that they are not throw-away or seen as project based. Going forward they need to be built into the organisations data integration approach.

Industry Standards

There are numerous organisations that publish standards on classification of drugs, illnesses etc and list of languages, currencies etc. It makes perfect sense to me that these standards are a good option rather than spending the energy managing the standard yourself. Obviously this does depend on what the standard is and why you need one.

I recently worked with a client that had a hotchpotch of ways of defining countries. They had some systems that used the ISO standard list of countries, but the majority used a variety of internally derived country lists. These lists included countries such as Yugoslavia and Central America. At that time Yugoslavia was no longer an individual country (due to a war) and Central America is clearly a region rather than a country. The sensible way forward was to make the ISO standard country list the master list (as it is world recognised, based upon the UN definition of countries and maintained by an organisation dedicated to such activities) and map everything to this one.

Standards aren't necessarily a solution on their own as there can often be competing standards. For example, a lack of consistency currently exists among different metadata standards. Dublin Core, for example, uses <label> as an identifier whilst USMARC uses <tag> , <indicator> and <subfield code>.

SME

Obtaining the expertise to resolve a crosswalk problem can be very problematic; as the reference lists themselves are often developed independently, and use different terminology, methods and processes.

You need to make use of your subject matter experts, as they will have a deeper understanding of the standard and also its back story. For example, the standard maybe being replaced soon or might have recently become the generally accepted option in the industry. There may be an industry standard that would be a better way forward than the existing reference values or there may be an existing mapping produced by a standards body.

Use the Enterprise Data Model

An enterprise data model can provide both an early warning system and a way of understanding the scope of the problem. We mentioned earlier about producing a mapping of all master data from our enterprise data model to all the logical level entities within each key database system. The identification and therefore early resolution management of crosswalks, can be one very useful area to apply that mapping. By knowing which master data (of type reference data) is held in which systems makes it possible to understand our reference data landscape. An understanding of the fundamental differences earlier in the process is advantageous over finding out when we try and actually integrate into the MDM process.

Data Governance

The last and by no means least approach to resolving crosswalks is the data governance process. By applying governance to the data aspects of system design we can reduce the introduction of differences in reference data values and definitions. This will result in, over time, the problem being reduced in scale, and possible even removed from the organisation (at least for some of the reference sets).

Summary

This chapter has explored the challenges faced when handling multiple sources of reference data. Sometimes it is not possible to link reference data together using a one-to-one mapping. The chapter has described the different types of collision points such as: definition, consistency, compound data types and history. It has also looked at a five point plan for how to address the crosswalk challenge.

10. Identity Management

Back in chapter 6 we looked at the authoritative source of data, and in chapter 7 and 8 we developed an understanding of how to find it and what to store it in. Now we need to start to understand how we construct our golden record within our golden source or Hub. In order to do this we need to bring the various records, from potentially quite disconnected systems, together and link them into one single record. This is one of the fundamental challenges with master data; how do we identify and link all our data together into a harmonised data set. In essence, how do we actually identify and match all the different records across all our systems to create our golden records. Without this we will never be able to truly gain the benefits of MDM such as the 360 view of customer, product or any other key data.

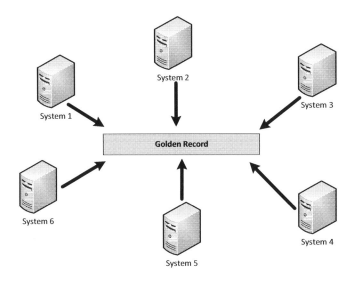

Figure 32 - The golden record

To address this problem we need to look at it from two angles - Identification and Record Linkage (or matching). This chapter addresses the identification challenge and the next chapter looks at how we match these records.

The Challenge of Identification

So let's start by looking at the problems associated with identification. Take customer identification, as an example. You would expect that every company, or organisation, would easily be able to identify its customers. Wouldn't this be quite a basic and fundamental capability for a business? Alas this is not the case.

In a business to business situation it is common to find that each division or local country operation may represent the same

119

customer company as different entries within the corporate or departmental CRM system. This can lead to fun when wanting to understand sales by customer; as you would need to identify all the companies that are actually the same and then roll up the figures. For example, we could have the following names for the same company (or parts of that company):

- ABC
- ABC Corporation
- ABC Plc
- A.B.C
- ABC Europe
- ABC Egypt
- ABC Property
- ABC Dynamics

It is not possible just from a name to be able to assume that companies are connected. ABC Europe and ABC Dynamics may in fact be completely different companies, with no connections whatsoever. On the other hand one may be a subsidiary of the other.

Within the consumer based world it's also common to exist as multiple contacts in a company's various systems; and even in multiple ways just in a single system. I often receive numerous emails from the same company about the same piece of direct marketing, but to different email addresses that I have. It would not be uncommon to have different entries in a CRM system for:

- John Smith
- Jonathan Smith
- J Smith
- John Smith
- Jon Smith

Then add into this confusion that you may be classified as a customer under one (or more) names, as a prospect under another and possibly as an ex-customer under a third. It could then get even more confusing as the customer may also be an employee. This would be common with mobile phone companies, banks, retail shops, etc.

Product is another good example. It can acquire many different identifiers depending on the part of the business or the point in its life cycle. Marketing may identify the product based upon its brand, whilst the manufacturing division would potentially use the Product Code and the retail outfit uses the SKU (Stock Keeping Unit). The lifecycle of a product also potential creates different identifiers for example; concept, production and post-production (ie after the company no longer sells it). Then we can confuse the situation even further by adding in products that are manufactured by multiple companies (to exactly the same spec). We could have four companies building a widget for company 'A' but company 'A' sells them as the same product to its customer.

Generally the problem of identifiers gets a little overlooked; as the assumption is that you just need to pick one and stick with it. This misses some of the fundamental issues such as the purpose of the identifier, politics and the shear cost, effort and complexity in conforming them all. Let's explore further the different types of identifiers and the role they all play.

Natural Identifiers/Identifying Attributes

The first set of identifiers to explore are the data's natural identifiers. Natural identifiers have actual real world meaning such as industry, government or other commonly accepted standards for identification. In order to try and explain the problem, let us look at employee identification as an example. In this area we would have a whole selection of identifiers to choose between, for example:

Identification Option	Authoritative Source
Full Name	Birth Certificate
National Insurance Number	UK Government
Network Username	Network Admin System
Employee Number	HR
Email address	Enterprise Email System

Figure 33 - Example identifiers

Of the five sources identified above, two are external and three are internal. It is common that many of the sources are external to an organisation. With this being the case it can become important to manage the relationship with the external data supplier.

Products have the same possibilities; for example financial products (stocks, bonds and other financial investment instruments) may have the following identifiers:

- CUSIP (Committee on Uniform Securities Identification Procedures) is a standard owned by the American Bankers Association and operated by Standard & Poor's.

- ISIN (International Securities Identification Number).

- SEDOL (Stock Exchange Daily Official List)

These standards include securities that do not have the identifiers from the other competing standards, but also do overlap so an investment may have a CUSIP, ISIN and SEDOL number. This creates problems for companies dealing in a wide range of securities, as it causes confusion. This type of cross reference problem between multiple identification schemes is very common, especially with Transaction Structure Data (e.g. Customer, Product, Outlet, etc) but can also exist with other forms of master data. On this journey of exploration that represents the search for an identifier for our master data, we find that it is typical to have competing identification schemes!

Keys

IT departments add to this confusion by introducing the concept of keys. Keys are IT terminology for a data attribute or group of data attributes that identify a collection of data items such as a database record. This is done for very practical reasons but does confuse the whole area as the subject of keys can create quite a barrier to non-database people. As a guide the following are the key pieces of terminology that should be understood:

- Natural key: This is an attribute (or set of attributes) that actually exist in the real world, and therefore have some level of business meaning. An example would be your tax number or employee number. General best

123

practice would guide you to not use the natural key as a unique identifier. The reasoning behind this is that the meaning and use of natural keys often becomes convoluted over time, for example you may get issued with a new tax number.

- Surrogate key: This is a system generated key that has no business meaning. It is used in databases to uniquely identify a single record. A generally excepted set of characteristics for a surrogate key would be:
    - Unique
    - System generated
    - Not null
    - Has no semantic meaning
- Primary key: The preferred attribute(s) to use to identify the individual unique records within the entity. A surrogate key is a primary key although a primary key doesn't have to always be a surrogate key. A generally excepted set of characteristics for a primary key would be:
    - Unique
    - Not null
- Alternate key: This is another attribute (or set of attributes) that can be used to identify a unique record within the entity. This is also referred to as the secondary key and is often a natural key.
- Foreign key: One or more attributes that can be used to link to another entity and a specific record within it. They will typically represent a primary key in the other entity.
- Composite key: A key that is composed of two or more attributes.

The Problem with Keys

Keys come with their own set of problems. Surrogate keys, for example, are identifiers for individual records in a database table, not for real things or people; therefore they have no implicit meaning in themselves. When data leaves any given application the value of the surrogate keys diminish rapidly. We cannot use them to identify if Customer A in one system is the same as Customer B in another. We are going to have to rely on other attributes of the customer.

Another problem with computer generated keys, such as surrogate and primary keys, are human beings. We are just not fantastic at using meaningless sets of numbers. They work great for computers but human beings need a bit of meaning embedded into the number. For example, a UK driving licence (actually the example is based upon England, Scotland and Wales) is made up of a 16 characters long unique code. The code is made up as follows:

Figure 34 - UK driving license code

1-5	The first five characters of the surname (padded with 9s if less than 5 characters)
6	The decade digit from the year of birth (e.g. for 1987 it would be 8)
7-8	The month of birth (7th character incremented by 5 if driver is female i.e. 51–62 instead of 01–12)
9-10	The date within the month of birth
11	The year digit from the year of birth (e.g. for 1987 it would be 7)
12-13	The first two initials of the first names, padded with a 9 if no middle name

14	Arbitrary digit – usually 9, but decremented to differentiate drivers with the first 13 characters in common
15-16	Two computer check digits.
17-18	Appended, two digits representing the license issue, which increases by 1 for each license issued.

By having some human comprehensible logic to it data quality, issues can be reduced.

When data leaves any given application the value of the surrogate keys diminish rapidly

---

Data Structure

The reality is that there is always going to be multiple identification schemes for a customer, product or any other master data. So what do we do about it? It is important that we find a mechanism for cross referencing the different identifiers. This also needs to bring them all together into a single identifier, that can be matched to all instances of the associated natural keys. The foundation to this is the data structure used to store the data in within our MDM hub. This needs to allow for all of these points.

In Figure 35, we have a fragment of a data model that can be used to manage this type of data.

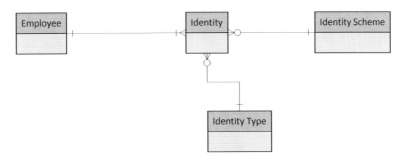

Figure 35 - Identity model fragment

The Identity Scheme table has one entry for each different scheme or standard that identifies an Employee; such as Tax Number, Full Name, Network Username etc. Because an employee can have more than one of these, we have an intersection table called Identity that can have multiple records per Employee. The Identity type can be used to classify schemes into different groups; maybe government identification, employer identification etc.

Summary

This chapter has focused on the identification attributes and the challenges associated with them. As we have seen it is not as easy as you might think to identify a customer, employee or product. Different ways of identifying each of these exist, but don't all align. We have also looked at computer generated ways of managing identification and to the advantages and disadvantages this brings.

11. Record Linkage

Record linkage refers to the act of finding records in one data set that match records in another. This is also called identity matching, data linkage, bridging, data matching, de-duplication and identity resolution. Direct mail companies refer to this process as list merging or list washing. Record linkage is necessary when joining data sets based on records that may or may not share a common identifier (e.g., surrogate key, name, email address or tax number).

It's Not Easy

Linking data from different sources of master data is not an easy task - in fact it can be downright difficult. The reasons for this are twofold:

- Master data is not always perfect! Fixing it all is an impossibility, so it is important to both understand this and have approaches for handling the problem.
- Data is complex! Different business rules, formats and data structures between different systems add to the complexity

Master Data is not Perfect

So the first question to ask ourselves is why is master data not perfect? The reality is that there may be nothing at all wrong with the data. For various business reasons the master data generated from one business process, that creates customer data, may differ (all be it ever so subtlety) from a second business process that creates customer master data. There could be legal or business reasons for the mis-match of master data. There could also be quality issues that have caused this dis-connect, sometimes technology based, sometimes process based and sometimes just caused by the practicalities of the situation. Records from different data sets may have differing identifiers (ie National Insurance Number in one and Employee Number in another).

Data has its own lifecycle and therefore changes over time. We move address, names often change with marriage, and lastly companies get brought and therefore change names and other data attributes.

In summary these differences exist for a reason, sometimes fixable and other times not. They are not going away anytime soon so need to be handled.

Data is Complex

Customer data can be very complex. A person's name, for example, may require many attributes to represent it. It would not be unreasonable to have the following attributes to represent a customer's name:

- Name prefix (Mr., Mrs., Dr., Captain)
- Given name (a.k.a. "first name" or "Christian name" in some cultures)
- Family name

- Middle name(s)
- Name Suffix (Jr., Sr., II, III)
- Initials
- Nickname
- Maiden name
- Married name
- Professional title
- Academic title

This type of data changes constantly. It would be typical of a customer's name that it could be stored in several different places: different departments, different locations, in different formats, etc.

Methods

So how do we link records from different sources together? In the next few pages we will look at the general process and some of the techniques.

As an overview the diagram below shows the general process that is followed. There is a pre-processing stage which addresses differences in format and structure, and also handles any data quality problems.

Then we get into the actual record matching activity, which looks at using a multitude of possible techniques called either rules based or fuzzy logic. The last process to identify is the reject handling activity which manages all rejected records.

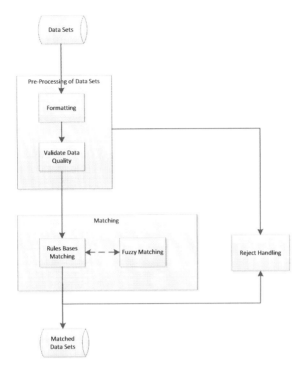

Figure 36 - Record Linkage process

It is important to note that different master data hub styles require different levels of matching, for example the Virtual Hub may require none.

Example

To work through the various stages of the matching process it helps to use an example. This will hopefully bring the process more to life. The example we are going to use is based upon a consumer based insurance organisation. We have two data sets (A and B) which come from presumable different policy management systems.

Figure 37 - Data Set A

Name	Sex	Date of Birth	Tax Number	Address
John Smith		1/3/1978	1234567	28 High Street, The Village, Kent
Peter Jones	Male	4/4/1967	2315667	11 Bird Close, Underbridge, Kent
Mary Smyth	Female	1/23/1971	9871235	2 The Street, The Village, Kent
Mr Hill	Male	1/3/1978	001234	25 High Street, The Village, Kent
J Smith	Male	1979	1134567	28 High Street, The Village, Kent

Figure 38 - Data Set B

Name	Sex	Year of Birth	Tax Number	Address
Jon Smith	M	1978		28 High Street, The Village, Kent
Peter Jones	M	67	2315667	11 Bird Close, Underbridge
Mary Smyth	F	1971		2 The Street, The Village, Kent
Mr Hill	M		001234	25 High Street, The Village, Kent
John Smyth	M		1134567	2 The Street, The Village, Kent

Pre Processing of Data Sets

Any kind of identity matching or data matching is very sensitive to the quality of the records being matched. It is therefore important to undertake some pre-processing to make sure that the quality and formatting of the data is as near to the same as possible.

Formatting

The level of accuracy of data matching will improve if records are all standardised; an example is the use of names. We may have a standard name format such as Title, First name and Surname. Standardisation can be easily handled through simple rule based data transformations. With our two data sets we have performed the following formatting transformations:

Data Set A

- The formatting of the attribute sex has been conformed to a standardised single letter, either 'M', 'F' or 'U'.

- The date of birth attribute for Mary Smyth has been fixed. It was detected that 01/23/1971 must be an American date format, so it has been converted to a UK format.

- We have created both first and surname attributes.

- A record ID has been created.

ID	First Name	Surname	Sex	Date of Birth	Year of Birth	Tax Number	Address
1	John	Smith	U	01/03/1978	1978	1234567	28 High Street, The Village, Kent
2	Peter	Jones	M	04/04/1967	1967	2315667	11 Bird Close, Underbridge, Kent
3	Mary	Smyth	F	23/01/1971	1971	9871235	2 The Street, The Village, Kent
4		Hill	M	01/03/1978	1978	001234	25 High Street, The Village, Kent
5	J	Smith	M		1979	1134567	7 The Street, The Village, Kent

Figure 39 - Data Set A after formatting stage

Data Set B

- The year of birth for Peter Jones has been fixed. It originally was 67 and has now been standardised to 1967 on the grounds that it is highly unlikely that the person was born in 1867?

- We have, as with data set A, created both first and surname attributes.

- A record ID has also been created as with data set A.

ID	First Name	Surname	Sex	Year of Birth	Tax Number	Address
1	Jon	Smith	M	1978		28 High Street, The Village, Kent
2	Peter	Jones	M	1967	2315667	11 Bird Close, Underbridge
3	Mary	Smyth	F	1971		2 The Street, The Village, Kent
4		Hill	M		001234	28 High Street, The Village, Kent
5	John	Smyth	M		1134567	7 The Street, The Village, Kent

Figure 40 - Data Set B after formatting stage

Validate Data Quality

The quality of the data also affects our ability to match data records. With our example data sets the following data quality checks and fixes have been performed:

- Data Set A, Record 1: Identified that John is typically a male name and therefore the unknown sex category is probably incorrect and should be changed to M.
- Data Set B, Record 2: Validated each of the addresses and identified that '11 Bird Close, Underbridge' is actually in Kent.

135

Figure 41 - Data Set A after DQ stage

ID	First Name	Surname	Sex	Date of Birth	Year of Birth	Tax Number	Address
1	John	Smith	M	1/3/1978	1978	1234567	28 High Street, The Village, Kent
2	Peter	Jones	M	4/4/1967	1967	2315667	11 Bird Close, Underbridge, Kent
3	Mary	Smyth	F	23/1/1971	1971	9871235	2 The Street, The Village, Kent
4		Hill	M	1/3/1978	1978	001234	28 High Street, The Village, Kent
5	J	Smith	M		1979	1134567	7 The Street, The Village, Kent

Figure 42 - Data Set B after DQ stage

ID	First Name	Surname	Sex	Year of Birth	Tax Number	Address
1	Jon	Smith	M	1978		28 High Street, The Village, Kent
2	Peter	Jones	M	1967	2315667	11 Bird Close, Underbridge, Kent
3	Mary	Smyth	F	1971		2 The Street, The Village, Kent
4		Hill	M		001234	25 High Street, The Village, Kent
5	John	Smyth	M		1134567	7 The Street, The Village, Kent

Matching

Matching falls into two basic approaches; either deterministic or probabilistic. Before exploring these approaches, we need to understand a few basics; such as the different roles attributes can be given in the match process and a few words about errors.

Attribute Categorisation

Attributes within the matching process can have a number of roles. It is therefore possible to group our attributes into three categories which are:

- Identities: These attributes, as we have discussed over the course of the last few chapters, are used to match records together.
- Discriminating: These attributes are used to rule out the matching of specific records. For example, if the date of birth is different in two different records they are likely not to be matched.
- Qualifying Attributes: These are used to identify the appropriate matching algorithm(s) to use. Examples would be: party type or attributes that identify the country etc.

Matching Errors

Two (or more) records incorrectly matched to the same master record are referred to as 'false positives'. Conversely the opposite ie two records not matched that should have been, are called 'false negatives'.

Some usage scenarios are actually quite tolerant of false positives, for example law enforcement. A detective wants to see all the suspects that meet his suspect profile, will expect to have a few false matches.

Rule Based Matching

Deterministic data matching, normally called rules based data matching, is the easiest to implement and understand. It is based on the idea that a number of identifying attributes must match in both data sets for any given records, before the conclusion can be reached that the records represent the same person or thing. This type of matching logic would also normally include a threshold. For example, if any two out of three identifiers match them we consider the records are matching. This is a very effective approach when the data sets being matched have a high number of identifiers such as names, date of birth and tax number.

Primary Match

The most simple deterministic record linkage strategy is to pick a single identifier that is assumed to be uniquely identifying, for example Tax Number, and assume that records with the same value identify the same person, while records not sharing the same value identify different people.

In our example, deterministic linkage based on Tax Number would create the following linkages:

- Data Set A, record 2 links to Data Set B, record 2
- Data Set A, record 4 links to Data Set B, record 4
- Data Set A, record 5 links to Data Set B, record 5

Secondary Match

A second round of rules may be declared that handles the exceptions from the primary matching rule. For example we might define that if the name, year of birth and address are the same then they are also the same person. Using this linkage method we would link: Data Set A, record 3 with Data Set B, record 3.

In our example this rule would still not match A1 with B1 because the names are still slightly different: standardisation put the names into the proper (Surname, Given name) format but could not discern "Jon" as a different spelling of "John". Running names through a phonetic algorithm such as Soundex, NYSIIS, or metaphone, can help to resolve these types of problems (though it may still stumble over surname changes as the result of marriage or divorce), and they are discussed in the fuzzy matching section below.

In can be seen from the example that data quality is important when it comes to rule based matching. A small degradation in quality will have a knock on effect to the level of matching.

Fuzzy Matching

The next approach is called fuzzy matching or probabilistic record linkage. This approach takes into account a larger set of identifiers. It uses a probability based method to identify matches, where the match outcome can be not only true or false but also a percentage of certainty; hence the name fuzzy.

By applying weighting and mathematical probability we can calculate if any two given records refer to the same thing (or person). For every set of data examined, the algorithm will give a probability score to determine the accuracy of the match.

A great example of this is the soundex function found in most database systems. In essence a soundex function returns a value that is based on how the string sounds when spoken. This is probably easier understood with some examples (using Transact-SQL).

If we take the names Jon Smith, John Smyth and John Schmidt we can perform a soundex on each half of the names and would come up with the following:

SELECT SOUNDEX ('Jon'), SOUNDEX ('John');

J500   J500

SELECT SOUNDEX ('Smith'), SOUNDEX ('Smyth'), SOUNDEX ('Schmidt');

S530   S530   S253

This means that of the three names two, based on the soundex function, seem to be similar sounding names (Jon Smith and John Smyth).

Name	First name	Surname	Match
Jon Smith	J500	S530	Yes
John Smyth	J500	S530	Yes
John Schmidt	J500	S253	No

Figure 43 - Soundex Example

Soundex is quite limited in its capability to identify similarities in words. Take for example Brighton and Bristol. If I run a soundex function on them I get B623 for both even though apart from the first three letters they have little similarity.

There are a wide variety of different algorithms that can be used in a fuzzy matching process. Appendix B provides an overview of these options.

140

Reconciliation Process

Now that we have managed to match all the records we have to start to deal with the contradictions in the data that are left over. An example would be record 1 in both data sets which has the following:

Attribute	Data Set A Value	Data Set B Value	Comments
First Name	John	Jon	Needs validating by possibly contacting the customer or checking our records
Surname	Smith	Smith	
Sex	M	M	
Date of Birth	1/3/1978		A wins
Year of Birth	1978	1978	
Tax Number	123456		A Wins
Address	28 High Street, The Village, Kent	28 High Street, The Village, Kent	

We have similar reconciliation required for other records which will need to be worked through.

Reject Handling

Rejected records will be put into a reject list and based on the reason for the rejection, they may be re-processed or reported as failed matches.

141

Matched Data Sets

For completeness I have included the final matching results from the two data sets below:

Figure 44 – Matched Data Set

ID	First Name	Surname	Sex	Date of Birth	Year of Birth	Tax Number	Address
1	John	Smith	M	01/03/1978	1978	1234567	28 High Street, The Village, Kent
2	Peter	Jones	M	04/04/1967	1967	2315667	11 Bird Close, Underbridge, Kent
3	Mary	Smyth	F	23/01/1971	1971	9871235	2 The Street, The Village, Kent
4		Hill	M	01/03/1978	1978	001234	28 High Street, The Village, Kent
5	J	Smith	M		1979	1134567	7 The Street, The Village, Kent

Additional Concepts

This chapter only scratches at the surface of the complexity that is faced in matching records. Before we end it a few other subjects need mentioning: granularity, thresholds and chaining.

Granularity

We also potentially need to handle granularity issues. Data that is at different levels of grain, caused by the way it is extracted from the source system, can be a major headache. This needs to be reconciled to be able to successfully match the records from both systems.

Thresholds

If the quality of a particular matching run is very poor, we would probably want to stop the run as the likelihood is that there are bigger problems. In fact we could find that continuing would actually cause more problems than it solved.

Determining when to stop the run is typically based on an error threshold. Where to set the threshold of match/non-match records is a bit of a balancing act, as you have to weigh up the acceptable level of sensitivity of the matching process.

Chaining

This is the process where records are matched to the master record via another record creating a chain. For example record 1 is our master record and if we are working on a matching rule that says three attributes must match as a minimum then we can match record 1 with record 2 (on the name, sex and tax number) and record 2 with record 3 (on the name, sex, date of birth and address)

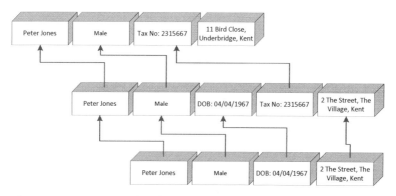

Figure 45 - An example of chaining

Summary

This chapter has looked at the process of matching records from different systems that are in fact about the same thing. As can be seen this is a complex problem and we are just scratching the surface. We have looked at the process involved, using both a deterministic matching process that is very logic driven to using probabilistic methods typically called fuzzy matching. This capability is a key requirement in any MDM architecture.

12. The Challenges of Global MDM

The world is now global and if your organisation wants to manage global data effectively, it will need to understand the nuances of data from all corners of the world. To put this into perspective, in the world today we have in excess of 200 countries speaking more than 10,000 languages and many different styles and formats for addresses. In this chapter I will try to give an introduction to a few of the areas you need to be mindful of when managing global master data.

Calendars

It's typical for western companies to make the assumption that the world all uses the same concept of time or calendars, but in fact there are a number of differences as you traverse the world. Even with the massive globalisation that has occurred over the last century there are still a number of calendars in use.

Gregorian Calendar

The Gregorian calendar is the de facto international standard and is used almost everywhere in the world for civil purposes. Due to the Gregorian calendar's obvious connotations of Western Christianity some non-Christians and even a few Christians replace the traditional "AD" and "BC" ("Anno Domini" and "Before Christ") notation with "CE" and "BCE" ("Common Era" and "Before Common Era").

Islamic Calendar

The Islamic calendar (Muslim or Hijri calendar) is a lunar calendar consisting of 12 lunar months in a year of 354 or 355 days. It is used to date events in most of the Muslim countries (concurrently with the Gregorian calendar), and used by Muslims everywhere to determine the proper day on which to celebrate Islamic holy days and festivals.

Hindu Calendar

The lunisolar Hindu calendars are some of the most ancient calendars of the world. The names of the twelve months are the same in most parts of India (because they are named in Sanskrit) though the spelling and pronunciation vary slightly and the first month of the year varies from one region to another depending upon past traditions. The standardised Indian national calendar based on Saka era with 78 CE as the start of the calendar is a lunar Hindu calendar used by the government together with Gregorian calendar. However, it is not used by the general public which widely uses the Vikrami lunar calendar Vikram Samvat with 56 BCE as the start of the calendar for religious activities and festivals. Vikram Samvat is also the official calendar in Nepal.

Julian Calendar

The Julian calendar, named after Julius Caesar, replaced the Roman calendar with the intention of creating a simplified and standardised one. It has a year of 365 days divided into 12 months with a leap day added to the month of February every four years. The calendar was used throughout the Roman Empire.

Due to a series of administration/calculation errors the calendar introduced anomalies. Every 128 years the year shifts one day backwards. The solution to this problem was, in 1582, to replace it with the Gregorian calendar.

Although the Gregorian calendar has become the international standard, the Julian calendar was still used up until the early 1900s. Some Orthodox churches still use it today; for example the Orthodox Church in Russia and the Berber people of North Africa.

Hebrew Calendar

While the Gregorian calendar is widely used in Israel's business and day-to-day affairs, the Hebrew calendar, used by Jews worldwide for religious and cultural affairs, also influences civil matters in Israel (such as national holidays) and can be used there for business dealings (such as for the dating of cheques).

Other Calendars

Other calendars also exist for example:

- The Iranian (Persian) calendar is used in Iran and some parts of Afghanistan.
- The Ethiopian calendar or Ethiopic calendar is the principal calendar used in Ethiopia and Eritrea, with the Oromo calendar also in use in some areas.

- In neighbouring Somalia, the Somali calendar co-exists alongside the Gregorian and Islamic calendars.
- In Thailand, where the Thai solar calendar is used, the months and days have adopted the western standard, although the years are still based on the traditional Buddhist calendar.

Fiscal Calendars

A fiscal calendar generally means the accounting year of a government or a business. It is used for budgeting, keeping accounts and taxation. It is a set of twelve months that may start at any date in a year, for example

- The US government's fiscal year starts on 1 October and ends on 30 September.
- The government of India's fiscal year starts on 1 April and ends on 31 March. Small traditional businesses in India start the fiscal year on Diwali festival and end the day before the next year's Diwali festival.
- In Iran, the fiscal year starts usually on 1 farvardin and concludes on 29 esfand using the Solar Hijri calendar which equates to the 21st March to the 20th March.
- The UK government's fiscal year starts on 1st April and ends on 31st March.

In accounting (and particularly accounting software), a fiscal calendar (such as a 4/4/5 calendar) fixes each month at a specific number of weeks to facilitate comparisons from month to month and year to year. January always has exactly 4 weeks (Sunday through Saturday), February has 4 weeks, March has 5 weeks, etc.

Seasons

In most parts of the world there are four seasons in a year: spring, summer, autumn (or fall US), and winter. In tropical and subtropical regions there are two seasons: the rainy (or wet, or monsoon) season and the dry season. This is because the rain changes more than the temperature. At any time, in any season, the northern and southern hemispheres (halves of the Earth) have opposite seasons.

Weekends

In most Western countries the working week is from Monday to Friday with Saturday and Sunday reserved for the weekend. Within the majority Muslim parts of the world the weekend is either Thursday to Friday or Friday to Saturday. The weekends in Israel are Friday to Saturday due to the Jewish Shabbat.

Addresses

One of the main pieces of data in any MDM rollout is locality, ie the physical address, postal address, and geographical data. Postal addresses can be particularly tricky as there is no internationally recognised standard address format. In almost every country, the address format differs. To show some of the differences I have included below some simple examples from around the world.

Figure 46 - USA Address format

1/ Recipient	John Smith
2/House Number and Street Name.	2101 MASSACHUSETTS AVE NW
3/ Locality, province and postal code	WASHINGTON DC 20008

Figure 47 - UK Address format

1/ Recipient	John Smith
2/House Number and Street Name.	1 Threadneedle Street
3/ Locality	London
4/ Postal code	EC2R 8AH

Figure 48 - French Address format

1/ Recipient	Jacques Smyth
2/House Number and Street Name.	21 ALLEE PICARD
3/ Postal Code and the locality	69200 VENISSIEUX

Figure 49 - Malaysia Address format

1/ Recipient	Si Anu
2/Street Name and the House	Jalan Ampang 1
3/ Postal Code and the locality	50450 KUALA LUMPUR
4/ Province	Wilayah Persekutuan

As can be seen from these examples the differences are quite evident. For example:

- The UK and USA position the postal code at the end of the address.
- Malaysia has the house number after the street name.

Names

Names are another example of a global inconsistency. If we look at Iceland, it is traditional to use the name of your father as the basis for your last name. The father's name is followed by 'sonur' or 'sson' for a boy and 'dottir' or 'sdóttir' for a girl. The last name is not typically used much as Icelanders prefer to be called by their given name, or by their full name. Telephone directories in Iceland are sorted by given name not last name. Other countries that also adopt a similar naming concept include: parts of Southern India, Malaysia and Indonesia.

In some countries such as China, Japan, Korea and Hungary it is common to have the family name as the first name. China also has a concept of a generation name which is normally after the family name but before the given name. In many Spanish-speaking countries people will often have two family names or possibly more.

There is a general assumption that members of the same family share the same family name but this is a dangerous assumption to make. There is a growing trend in the West for wives to keep their own name after marriage. It is also possible that the same person could be registered under a family name and a professional name because they didn't change their professional name after marriage.

Data Privacy

Data Privacy laws vary across the globe. What you can do with an individual's data in one jurisdiction may be quite different from what you can do in another. Just look at all the interesting battles that are occurring with some of the US owned internet businesses and European legislators over recent years. This is a challenging area and requires legal advice before making any concrete decisions. To give a few examples of the general differences:

- In the United States, the US Patriot Act allows the government to demand access to the data stored on any computer.
- In the United Kingdom: The Information Commissioner can impose fines of up to GBP 500,000 for serious breaches of the Act. Financial services firms regulated by the Financial Conduct Authority ("FCA") may find that a breach of the Act may also give rise to enforcement action by the FCA in respect of a breach of the FCA Principles for Business. The FCA enforcement powers are extensive and can include unlimited fines.
- In France the CNIL has the power to order a financial sanction up to EUR 150,000 for the first violation, and further fines for subsequent violations. It is also possible that a violation may constitute a misdemeanor and in that case would be punishable by up to 5 years' imprisonment.

A great site to get a general overview of the state of data privacy around the world is the DLA Piper data protection site (http://dlapiperdataprotection.com/#handbook/world-map-section). I have only ever used the website as a general piece of background, so have no idea of the quality of any products they

152

may sell. Please don't take this recommendation as anything other than just a great site to browse.

Summary

Master data management is a global activity and it is important to understand what that means. We forget that different countries have quite different cultural perspectives and traditions, and these have impact on how we manage our master data. In this chapter we have learnt that time, addresses, name and data privacy all play a part in the rich levels of diversity we are going to encounter.

13. Project Challenges

We have spent time exploring what MDM is, and what's involved in building an architecture; whether that be process or system based (or in reality probably a mixture of the two). In this last chapter it is appropriate that we turn our attention to some of the organisational and project based challenges associated with making this happen.

What's the use of running if you are not on the right road.

These challenges can be grouped into three buckets of subjects:

- Hearts and Minds
- Governance & Organisation
- Technology

Hearts and Minds

To win the hearts and minds of the organisation any project, or programme, will need to do a lot of stakeholder management. To be successful you need to have a vision and be able to show progress. This is even more critical to MDM initiatives because as mentioned in Chapter 3, IT have been very good at hiding the problems we are looking at resolving.

Vision

An MDM initiative needs a vision that articulates what MDM means for your organisation, and why you need it. This vision needs to map onto the company's business vision and provide the light that shows the way. There is a German proverb that I've used a few times, which summarises this and goes "What's the use of running if you are not on the right road".

Strategy

The strategy is about how the vision becomes reality. It takes you through the journey that is needed to reach the end goal and along the way provides the direction and guidance to the various decisions that will need to be made. It is about knowing what good looks like, and to be able to measure progress towards those goals.

A strategy is never a finished document but instead is a continuously evolving architectural product. Key areas that need to be covered within the strategy are the:

- Business drivers that highlight what the problem means to the business in a language that they can understand.

- Current and future states of the technology and organisational landscape.
- Roadmap of how we are going to get from the current state to the future state and the various transition states along the way.

Measure

Define the expected results and set up measurements for them early on. Master data ownership and data quality have a high emotional power. Measuring and communication of results is essential to bring the conversation to facts, and be able to link to business value. It is important to concentrate on the metrics to which business stakeholders pay the most attention.

Governance & Organisation

All successful organisations need the individuals within to pull together to achieve objectives. If an organisation grows too large or too complex this becomes difficult to achieve effectively. Governance is an effective mechanism for facilitating this. It is the process through which groups make decisions that direct their collective efforts.

Data governance allows us to add rigor and discipline to managing, using, improving and protecting our organisations data assets. If implemented correctly it can enhance the quality, integration and availability of data by allowing a greater degree of data harmony across the organisation. If implemented badly, it creates a bureaucratic nightmare of standards and red tape.

MDM and data governance have far more in common that at first may be apparent, as they have grown out of the same set of organisational issues. Organisations need to have control over the rapidly growing volumes of key business data, such as customers, suppliers and product and both MDM and data governance are trying to address this. Even through the challenges they are resolving are the same, they have grown up rather independently. MDM went down the technology route and data governance went down the organisational route. This relates back to my comments earlier in this book about MDM not being just a technology. MDM can be achieved by processes alone, ie governance. Clearly the optimal result is a health mix of the two.

Technology

In this section I didn't want to write about the technology per say but look at a few important considerations when deciding on technological solves.

- Don't focus on the technology but instead understand the value it provides. As technologists we get excited by new gadgets and can get hypnotised by the flashing lights. These desires need to be managed.
- Should we build the solution or buy in a software package? The whole build vs buy debate is important because buying can be a fantastic cost effective and high quality way forward but not always. Weigh up the pros and cons of both approaches based upon what is available in the marketplace at the time, the practicalities of what you are doing and your technical perfectionism and idealism.
- Manage your master data based upon the value it provides. MDM processes and technologies can be

expensive in terms of resources and time as well as the obvious cost impact. Master data should be managed proportionally with potentially different levels of sophistication depending on the master data. In essence I am recommending that master data should be graded as regards value to the business and managed accordingly.

- Watch out for the MDM salesman (or woman). Buy what's good for your company not what's good for the sales person's commission cheque.

Maturity

In order to assess the maturity of an organisations MDM capability we need something to measure ourselves against. A maturity model makes it possible to measure the level of MDM capability within organisations, based upon a standard framework. The diagram below shows an example of a typical MDM maturity model.

At the start of a MDM project, the ambition level should be set indicating what maturity level the organisation aims to reach. This gives us a target to work towards and stops the whole MDM problem looking like an impossible mountain to climb.

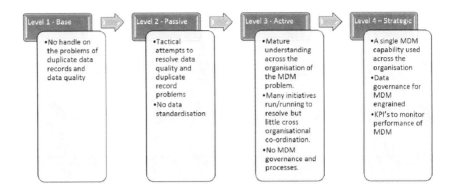

Figure 50 - Maturity Model

Free Downloads

There are a few, hopefully useful utilities, which can be down loaded for free via the following link: www.koios-associates.com/MDMdownload.htm.

Summary

In the last chapter we have briefly looked at the three key areas associated with successful implementation of MDM:

- Hearts and minds: This is all about explaining why we are going to undertake this initiative and how we are going to approach the problem.

- Governance & Organisation: It is important to make sure the organisation has the right organisational rigor and discipline to ensure we get maximum value from our master data.
- Technology: Lastly the technology considerations that underpins the delivery of our MDM capability.

References

[1] One of the classic images of a sea monster on a map: a giant sea-serpent attacks a ship off the coast of Norway on Olaus Magnus's Carta marina of 1539. This image is from the 1572 edition and is from the National Library of Sweden.

Sea Monsters were drawn on maps for many reasons other than to just scare the reader. Reasons included:

- The weird bestiary at the edges of maps was in large part an artistic decision, a chance for cartographers to fill in ugly white spaces of the still-unexplored Earth and to stretch their creative wings.
- To deter and obfuscate. Sailors, who had discovered a new route, wanted to keep others away and made up terrible reports.
- But they also served as a reminder of the very real dangers faced by the explorers of the day. No one knew what was out there, and many who left didn't come back.

[2] The 10 day MBA by Steven Silbiger. I've an old copy from the mid 90's that this note relates to.

[3] This quote is actually taken from the BBC website and an article about the BBC's Money programme by John Penycate. http://news.bbc.co.uk/1/hi/uk/1395109.stm

[4] The Stone of the Philosophers by Edward Kelly

This is ascribed to Edward Kelly and included in Tractatus duo egregii, de Lapide Philosophorum, una cum Theatro astronomiæ terrestri, cum Figuris, in gratiam filiorum Hermetis nunc primum in lucem editi, curante J. L.M.C. [Johanne Lange Medicin Candidato]., Hamburg, 1676.

This version has been transcribed by L. Roberts

http://www.alchemywebsite.com/kellystn.html

[5] Taken from the EMC report '2011 Digital Universe Study: Extracting Value from Chaos'.

Fuzzy Matching Algorithms

This appendix lists out some of the matching algorithms that fall under the label of 'fuzzy matching algorithms'. They are listed for background information and not as an authoritative source. It would be expected that further investigation would be undertaken by the reader prior to making use of them.

Phonetic Matching

This method detects like sounding relationships between words and has now typically replaced the 'Soundex' matching algorithm. As an example, phonetic matching will identify a sound-alike relationship between 'Jon' and 'John' but no relationship between 'Fred' and 'Ginger.'

'Near' Algorithms

These algorithms are used when matching words that have a few potential typographical errors.

- Fast Near
- Accurate Near
- Frequency Near

'Only' Algorithms

This is a set of different but similar matching algorithms.

- Alphas Only: Sometimes extra characters and numbers confuse the matching process. For example Freds and Fred's may actually represent the same thing but the grammar can get in the way. The 'Alphas Only' algorithm ignores these extra characters and as its names suggested only compares the alphabetic characters.
- Consonants Only: Only the consonants will be compared (see 'Alphas Only').
- Numeric's Only: Only the numeric characters will be compared (see 'Alphas Only').
- Vowels Only: Only the vowels will be compared (see 'Alphas Only').

'Distance' Algorithms

These algorithms measures the number of substitutions required to change one into the other ie the distance between the strings.

- Hamming distance
- Levenshtein distance
- Needleman-Wunch distance or Sellers Algorithm: Has a cocepts of cost adjustment to the distance.
- Smith-Waterman distance: Also has a cost concept with two adjustable parameters.
- Gotoh Distance or Smith-Waterman-Gotoh distance:
- Jaro and Jaro Winkler

Others

Levenshtein Containment:

Matches when one record's component is contained in another record.

Cosine similarity

Used in text mining to ascertain the level of similarity of documents.

N-gram or Q-gram-based Algorithms

Used to count the frequency of words appearing together in a fixed order.

Naïve bayes

The algorithm classifies an item or piece of text based upon particular features.

Frequency

Matches the characters in one piece of text to another without any regard to the sequence of characters.

The Silk Road Story

To explain the MDM challenge in non IT terms I have included below the story of 'The Silk Road' as it provides an approximation of the issue but set within a historical context. This text is actually borrowed from a previous book of mine but felt it was useful for those that haven't seen it before.

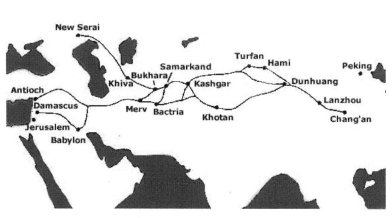

Figure 51 - The Silk Road

The Silk Road is an extensive interconnected network of trade routes across the Asian continent that connects Asia with the Mediterranean and Africa. The description of this route as the `Silk Road' is somewhat misleading. Firstly, although the word road implies a continuous journey, very few travellers traversed the route from end to end. Typically, goods passed through a series of agents. Secondly, no single route was taken; crossing Central Asia several different branches developed. Extending for over 4,000 miles this route was not only a conduit for silk, but also for many other products.

The route was extremely treacherous. The Chinese monk, Faxian, gives us an inkling from the accounts of his travels along the road at the end of the fourth century:

"The only road-signs are the skeletons of the dead. Wherever they lie, there lies the road to India." Faxian, 399 to 414 BC

As has been mentioned silk wasn't the only precious commodity traded. Caravans heading towards China carried gold and other precious metals, ivory, precious stones, and glass, which were not manufactured in China at that time. In the opposite direction furs, ceramics, jade, bronze objects, lacquer and iron were traded. Many of these goods were bartered for others along the way, and objects often changed hands many times. There are no records of Roman traders being seen in China, nor Chinese merchants in Rome. In essence silk passed from China to Rome through many agents meaning that:

- The Chinese never knew where the silk went
- The Romans never knew where it came from

This is the crux of the MDM problem:

- The Data Producers never know who is using their data
- The Data Consumers never know where their data comes from

Index

Index

Made in the USA
Lexington, KY
16 April 2015